Christi␣␣Lamb has come to a␣␣␣␣␣␣␣␣␣␣in life. Her first two books ␣␣e written in while she was in her 80s – *From The Ends of the E␣␣th – passionate plant collectors remembered in a Cornish garden␣*␣ene Factum 2004) and her WW2 memoir *I Only Joined for the␣␣Iat...Redoubtable Wrens at War...their trials, tribulations ␣␣! triumphs* (Bene Factum 2007). She then celebrated her 90th bi␣␣iday by penning *This Infant Adventure – Offspring of the Roya␣␣irdens at Kew* (Bene Factum 2010).

As␣␣␣ssionate plantswoman Christian is a Fellow of the Linna␣␣␣ociety, an inquisitive historian, and an insatiable traveller␣␣many years she lived in Cornwall where her garden, and t␣␣␣␣its in it, reflected her heroes – the original plant collectors w␣␣␣ought back the original plant specimens from the furthest c␣␣␣␣s of the world. She now lives in London overlooking the Thar␣␣s.

:hristianlamb.co.uk

CRUISING ALONG

AROUND THE WORLD IN EIGHTY YEARS

Christian Lamb

Bene Factum Publishing

Cruising Along
Published in 2014 by
Bene Factum Publishing Ltd
PO Box 58122
London
SW8 5WZ
inquiries@bene-factum.co.uk
www.bene-factum.co.uk

Print Edition ISBN: 978-1-909657-71-7
Epub ISBN: 978-1-909657-72-4
PRC/MOBI ISBN: 978-1-909657-73-1

A CIP catalogue record of this is available from the British Library.

Cover design and illustration: Tony Hannaford
Typesetting: Tony Hannaford

Printed and bound in the UK

Contents

Acknowledgements

My thanks for so many enjoyable cruises over the last eighty years must go out to many people who sadly I am unable to name – they are the captains and the crews of the many vessels on which I've sailed, and also my fellow passengers and travelling companions. Without you all this book could not have been launched.

However, there are others who I can acknowledge by name and to whom I extend my appreciation.

My most recent voyages have been wonderfully organised by cruise specialist Amelia Dalton *(www.ameliadaltontravel.co.uk)* and so my first thanks must go her.

My eldest grandson, Jamie Rollo, coincidentally happens to be Head of Travel and Leisure for Morgan Stanley; his input and advice have been extremely useful.

Others include various authors who have informed and inspired me, and in some cases from whom I quote here in my own book. These include Meriel Larken (*The Ship, The Lady and The Lake*, Bene Factum Publishing 2012), Hugh Low (*Diaries 1844-1846*, most recently published by Natural History Publications (Borneo 2002), Robert Fortune (*Three Years Wandering in China*, first published in 1847 by John Murray), and Colonel J. H. Williams (*Elephant Bill*, first published in 1950 by Rupert Hart-Davis).

Thanks also to Mike Phillips who from the far reaches of Cornwall continues to advise me and keep my wilful computer fully functioning up here in London.

And finally my gratitude goes to Anthony Weldon and Dominic Horsfall of Bene Factum for their excellent editing and expertise in producing this book, and to Tony Hannaford for the design and the iconic cover.

Christian Lamb
London 2014

CRUISING ALONG

AROUND THE WORLD IN EIGHTY YEARS

Introduction

It seems the blackest irony that the terrible disaster which struck the *Titanic* could have been the catalyst which launched this desirable mirage. Her unlucky encounter with the iceberg and subsequent sinking, with such loss of life, so dramatically reproduced in the film, could never be forgotten, but neither could her glamour; she had been built as the largest and fastest ship afloat – advertised as unsinkable – she was a legend even before she sailed. White Star Line, later Cunard, had spared no expense in assuring her luxury and safety – so sure were they of this that they provided only the number of lifeboats specified by the Board of Trade, which as we all know was woefully short; her 2,200 passengers were a mixture of the world's wealthiest, glorying in the elegance of First Class accommodation, and immigrants packed into steerage. In her day – 1912 – before the First World War, cruising for pleasure was a new idea, then just catching on; travelling had always been a dour and sometimes dangerous means to an end, a necessary way of getting from A to B; soldiers, civil servants and very often their families had to get to the far flung parts of the British Empire; also travel arrangements made for their many friends and relations, who became known as the fishing fleet (the young females following hopefully, very often after suitable young men to marry). It was many years before people began to think of ships as anything but means of transport. But now *Titanic* was part of history, an epic never to be erased from one's memory; but rather like some of the horrors of war, the desperate pictures began to fade, and as crossing the Atlantic became a frequent necessity, Cunard seized the opportunity to tempt the rich and famous once again.

The *Queen Mary* was built for the sprint between Southampton and New York; she was an immediate success and won the prestigious Blue Riband; this was the most coveted trophy afloat and was first won by *Scotia* in 1862 at the average speed of 15 knots; it was a race across the Atlantic and was won by Cunard off and on for the next 100 years. In 1938 she still won the Blue Riband at 31.69 knots, but lost it in 1952 to *United States* at 35.59 knots.

The grandeur of the *Queen Mary* was provided by her architects who chose Art Deco for her background theme, vast arched saloons, specially woven carpets and beautiful furniture – the First Class cabins were out of this world; special woods from different parts of the British Empire were chosen for the furnishings of the staterooms; it was noted with some amazement that after the ship docked, not a single ashtray was left on board – such was the popularity of these much coveted items as souvenirs.

It was in the early 1930s that the golden age of liners began. The French Government subsidised the building of the *Normondie*, which wrested the Blue Riband from the *Queen Mary* several years running and took her place as the largest and fastest, and with her desirable Gallic culture boasted an almost intimidating formal nobility.

During the late thirties cruising was being aimed more at the middle classes and became the height of fashion, almost a status symbol; you could spend a dollop of your retirement pension on a three-month voyage, which would take you round the world and back again. It was an opportunity to take part in this national sport, showing off your wife's ravishing wardrobe of the latest, up to the minute, brand new fashion, while she vied with her friends to have the most unbelievable amount of elegant, matching luggage. Enterprising ships took to the warmer waters of the Mediterranean, Cunard had the Atlantic to themselves and spread the aspiration that Britannia still ruled the waves. Sunbathing by the pool, deck games, bingo, hairdressing, massage parlours, it was all there for you. Then of course came World War 2 and the end of such frivolities.

It was at that moment that our 'monsters', as these capacious liners were called, came into their own, crossing the Atlantic at 26 knots, uniquely carrying whole divisions of troops; they were never once attacked by U-boats – this use of their speed and size made them unassailable. Serving as a member of the Women's Royal Naval Service (WRNS) myself, it was my job at Combined Services Headquarters at Plymouth to plot these huge ships with their precious cargo across the ocean, and on board many of them were other Wrens running the signals office, in constant touch with Bletchley Park, who would warn them of any dangers ahead or any change of course necessary. Americans took this lesson to heart and any large liner built after the war would be designed with the possibility of being turned into a hospital or troopship if required. The *United States*, built with this transport potential, was the biggest and fastest ever, and stole ten hours off the Blue Riband record.

It took a good few years after the war for anyone to think of holidays; but as rationing came to an end and thoughts of such pleasures began to pick up, and having endured one of the coldest winters on record, 'abroad' sounded attractive. The well-known

English belief that 'Dagoes begin at Calais' began to be questioned for the first time. Soon flying became safer and cheaper, and package holidays started to take hold; as the prices came down, almost anyone could afford a week in Benidorm or on a Spanish Costa, and an impressive tan to prove it. Then cruise ships began to reappear.

LEARNING TO CRUISE

Perhaps I first became seduced into cruising when an eccentric friend invited me in the early seventies to go with her on the fairly new *Queen Elizabeth 2* (Cunard's flagship had launched in 1969); a quick dash there and back, all because she fancied having lunch in the restaurant at the top of the Twin Towers in New York, and I fell for this super plan with alacrity. There was a slight hitch when the restaurant turned out to have a private membership, but the Manager very decently waived the subscription when he heard we were only there for the day. The *QE II* was no ordinary liner – she was known to be the most beautiful ship in the world, romantically called the 'Empress of the Sea', with the most elegant bow profile ever conceived; she was built on the Clyde by John Brown in 1967. During her 42-year reign she crossed the Atlantic 800 times; many of her passengers had a love affair with her, booking the same cabin time after time, knowing that they would be remembered and welcomed on board by the Cruise Manager, even after only one voyage, as if they were members of some exclusive club, and greeted by the same devoted stewards.

With such a build-up it was quite exciting anticipating what to expect. The captain's cocktail party was one of the highlights – one could only gasp at the extreme outfits and hats some of the ladies sported. Lunch was my favourite meal when caviar was served as a main course. Whatever you wanted for dinner would be produced, even if it was not on the menu.

Watching from the bridge as one came up the Hudson River on the way to New York at 5 am, just as the sun rose and the sky turned from night into day, sailing past the enormous Statue of Liberty, was a historic moment – this had been a gift of friendship from the people of France to the United States and is recognised as a universal symbol of freedom and democracy, dedicated as such on 28th October 1886.

There was time on arrival to take a stretch limo down Wall Street and other places of note, before being transported up in the Twin Towers' vast lift, which could easily accommodate 100 people, and which took about ten seconds to waft you to the top (107th floor – one's stomach seemed to remain at ground level) where the whole of New York lay before you. The view from the restaurant extended along the south side of the World Trade Centre as well as the corner over part of the east side. Looking out from the bar through the full-length windows, the stunning picture of the southern tip of Manhattan, where the Hudson and East rivers meet, was visible. In addition one could see the Liberty State Park, Ellis Island and Staten Island with the Verrazano-Narrows Bridge. All in all a sombre recollection, never to be forgotten by those lucky enough to have seen it. Hardly had you recovered from all this when you would have the return voyage and all the trimmings to look forward to.

Aged 8 and almost ready for a lifetime of cruises.

Until aeroplanes became the norm, everybody travelled by sea; it was an adventure, but long journeys were not always anticipated with pleasure. *Mal-de-mer* was quite a serious illness for some people, and no panaceas such as pills and patches were then on offer.

HMS Shropshire – the County-class cruiser captained by my father in 1930.

My first encounter with such travel was in 1930 when I was ten; my father had been appointed Captain of the County-class cruiser HMS *Shropshire* to join His Majesty's Mediterranean Fleet stationed in Malta; my mother booked us all (one paid for oneself in those days) – my sister Anne, aged 11, brother Francis, aged seven, and our governess Miss de Grey, who actually lived in Malta as her father was head of the police there – on a fairly ordinary ship, not equipped for pleasure, as I remember the *Ranpura*. She was built as an ocean liner for the Peninsular and Oriental Steam Navigation Company in 1924 and was the first P&O 'R' Class liner to have her interior designed by Lord Inchcape's daughter, Elsie Mackay. In 1936, while transporting $50 million worth of Chinese artwork from London to Shanghai, she encountered a storm on her way to Gibraltar and ran aground off Punta Mala after dragging her anchor; luckily she was refloated without damage, resuming her trip to China.

We sailed from Southampton in great excitement – it was very rough in the Bay of Biscay, famous for its storms, and often a sick-making experience for those new to sailing; an added drama was a ship in distress on our route, and we were ordered to keep her company until she could be taken in tow; Anne and I seemed to be the only passengers who appeared regularly for meals, and with the ship apparently empty of other people we had a high old time tearing round amusing ourselves.

We lived in Malta – the Mediterranean island famed for its bells, yells and smells – in astonishing luxury; everything was remarkably cheap. We had a cook and several maids, even a chauffeur, though he did have bare feet. He was called Edward and often drove us to parties.

The social life was a complete whirl with the Royal Navy at its zenith; young as I was, I remember watching the Fleet sail past from the breakwater of the Grand Harbour: there were numerous battle ships and battle cruisers, aircraft carriers (two of them called *Glorious* and *Furious*), my father's three-funnelled cruiser HMS *Shropshire*, HMS *London* – the Flagship – and HMS *Devonshire* of the same class, a great many destroyers, frigates, minesweepers and other vessels – it was some sight. The parties were endless, with so many ships – the perfect backdrop for dining and dancing; I recollect watching my father dressed as a Chinese for a fancy-dress affair, having his face made up. The entertainment was fun, even for children – the sailors loved them and dressed up as pirates, and would give us all rides in the ammunition lifts that fed the 15-inch guns. Three times a week, Anne and I were driven at 6 am, when it was cool, to our riding lessons, in a garry (horse-drawn carriage) from Guardamangia, our village, across the countryside to the Marsa, which was famous for its racing and polo matches. I learned to ride on David Niven's polo pony – he was then only a subaltern in the HLI (Highland Light Infantry), long before he became a film star. Our governess did her best to infiltrate this social scene by pursuing desirable young ship's officers, who it

I learnt to ride in Malta on David Niven's polo pony.

With my sister Anne.

was reputed had to batten themselves down under the hatches to escape.

A few years went by before my next serious voyage, in 1950 when my husband John, also in the Royal Navy, was sent off to Singapore to join the staff of the Commander in Chief. Following him, I travelled with our three children, aged five, three, and three months (Felicity, Simon and Martin), in a troopship called the *Empire Orwell*. She had been built by the Germans as a 'Strength through Joy' liner – '*Kraft durch Freude*', a German National Socialist Organisation – designed for providing cruises, concerts and cultural activities for the German workforce, especially directed towards the working class. A fleet of much subsidised KdF liners became wildly popular for the average German to enjoy in his free time.

These were removed by us at the end of the war and refitted to suit our requirements; this was no luxury cruise, and our small cabin consisted of two bunks, one above the other, the top one for me and the other for Felicity and Simon, supposedly sleeping heads and tails, with the baby (Martin) in a cot attached to their lower bunk. I considered this a recipe for murder and made my way up to the Officer in Command to ask if there was any way we could have a larger cabin. It took some time and several reminders – in fact, as I recall, we went on hunger strike for several days – before two doctors who were sharing a three-berth cabin were ordered to exchange with us and reluctantly obeyed, but they had their revenge later. All the senior officers travelling with their wives and children had nannies, but the latter were usually the first casualties of seasickness, so were more of a liability in the event. I think I was the only naval wife on board. Meals were a nightmare – we had eleven every day – the baby had five and the children and I three each, all at different times. I got better organised towards the end of the voyage when the OinC invited me to have a drink with him before the second sitting for dinner and then leave my youngest, Martin, in his cabin while I dined; this ensured he was not left to the mercy of my other children, supposed to be going to sleep. We were allowed ashore at Port Said and I spent time hunting for a camel to show the children, which eventually we found and had our photos taken sitting astride. I needn't have bothered, as sailing down the Suez Canal there were lots more camels with enchanting babies on either side – so close we could almost touch them. The next excitement was the ship breaking down in the Great Bitter Lake, and while she wallowed about we were invited to swim; I managed to find an under-employed nanny to guard my children while I indulged in the lake waters, which had the consistency of hot milk.

The children thought the whole expedition enormous fun and, having breakfast on deck as a special treat, insisted on eating porridge – this was in August with a following wind in the Red Sea; thus it wasn't long before they came out in spots and the re-located doctors had their revenge, painting the children purple with gentian violet (the cure-all for everything in those days), so sadly they looked anything but their best when we were invited by kind friends to go ashore in Colombo.

Three years later, at the end of the appointment, we all travelled back to England in two consecutive troopships, the children all being vertical by now; at the end of the first stage we broke the journey for a month's holiday in Ceylon (now Sri Lanka), taking a house up in the hills; it was quite exciting travelling in sleepers on this very old train, full of cockroaches, and with a somewhat doubtful dining car; sadly we journeyed overnight so were unable to see the wild elephants which live in that wooded country. The bungalow we had rented came complete with a cook and members of staff, all who adored and loved looking after children. I had been used to our Chinese cook and his wife in Singapore, who had kept the kitchen immaculately clean, so I made the mistake of visiting these kitchen premises – something I decided not to do again. The interesting plumbing was dependent on 'Dan Dan the lavatory man' (an old established Indian method of dealing with such things), who came round daily. The house was surrounded with heavenly hills, a splendid garden, and buses to take us anywhere we wanted to go. We did take one perilous trip (leaving the children with the kindly Indian staff) through several mountain ranges to Kandy and the Temple of the Sacred Tooth; there were narrow steep roads with cliff-hanger borders and endless hairpin bends, which very nearly caused even me to feel a certain *mal-de-mer*. Another day we spent with friends who were tea planters, and exploring their estate, we came across leeches; surprised to find my socks covered in blood, I noticed a nasty little black creature on Felicity's leg and pointed it out to our host – he spiked it rather fiercely and painfully (for Felicity and also for the leech, I hope) with his fag-end, causing it to fall off.

All too soon it was time to catch our next ship for the second half of our return journey, a voyage which included Christmas – never has the season been more delightfully and effortlessly (on our part) celebrated, with everything provided: Father Christmas, turkey, plum pudding, parties, tree – even presents. England awaited with January weather, no Chinese or Indian cooks or nannies, and thick clothes, all of which we had forgotten about and which occupied much of the day taking on and off.

ANCIENT HISTORY
IN THE
EASTERN MED

My voyage on the *QE II* might have given me delusions of grandeur but I knew very well that my first venture on an ordinary cruise ship would bear little resemblance. My friend Rosie Baldwin had asked me if I thought camellias would grow in Turkey – it occurred to me to go and find out. I knew that some varieties tolerate sun better than others, so I suggested half a dozen or so which she decided to take out with her and plant as an experiment and which I could later inspect when visiting her. Rosie lived in a rather nasty little cottage near me in Cornwall, but she also lived quite a lot in Turkey, and sometimes with her daughter in Majorca. She was much in demand, having lived through three husbands with many friends in different parts of Europe, and until you got to know her well, you might think she was name-dropping, but actually she only seemed to know people of note. Her Mini car was provided and replaced from time to time by the Agnelli family (inventers of Fiat) – she was an appalling driver and had to negotiate a difficult little Cornish lane on her way home. With Rosie's camellias as a good excuse, I started investigating cruises in the Mediterranean. I hoped to find a small ship with like-minded people, because by this time John had sadly died, so I would be travelling solo. I was really quite used to this anyway, because it is in the nature of a sailor that his ship and the exigencies of the Service come first, so one learns to do without help when it comes to carrying luggage, babies or the luxury of being met on arrival. Although it is never much fun being on your own to begin with, I had become extremely used to overcoming these initial hurdles, all of which stood me in good stead. Confucius recommends: *'He travels fastest who travels alone'*.

Swan Hellenic seemed to have the edge – ships not too enormous, interesting lectures, possibly congenial passengers; they offered me a place on a voyage which began in Venice in June, visiting places I wanted to see. It was pouring with rain when I arrived in Venice but I managed to have the ritual ice cream (costing an exorbitant £8) sitting under an umbrella on Saint Mark's Square. I was not surprised to find the *Orpheus* something of an old hulk and my cabin poky and creaky and rather cold. I found it impossible to turn off the air-conditioning (husbands are so much better at this sort of thing); I had packed in an optimistic way (as usual), with clothes more suitable for the Caribbean.

Swan Hellenic is rightly dedicated to showing their passengers everything of note, which in this magical area of ancient history was no easy task. The cruise wasn't meant to be a holiday, but I didn't know that. Keeping up with the schedule was quite an ordeal; I am allergic to herding or being packaged, so a typical day of terror for me started at cockcrow with instructions to disembark and join one of at least six identical buses, each with a local guide. I tried to follow Maria, an excellent girl who I had already met, but somehow I got involved with the naughty elderlies who had forgotten their number tag – a tiny little label without which one could neither land nor re-embark (raising nightmare visions of being left on the quay as the ship sailed away).

The cruise director, Doreen Goodrich, deserves a paragraph

to herself – she was a remarkable and valuable lady with organisational abilities to rival Napoleon. Wherever there was a bottleneck, trouble-shooter Doreen would be there. I heard one story of her in the Lebanon, when the buses were suddenly banned from the chosen route, but Doreen hired 110 taxis and rationed the passengers to four in each – no one was left behind and all returned in time. Doreen has the knack of scenting a crisis well in advance – she told me of another terrible day when the new cruise passengers were early and the homeward bound ones late; she had to arrange buses to drive round and round the countryside, filling in time, return the old passengers to Orpheus and give them lunch, finally sorting them all out to their correct destinations. You are not going to find many Doreens to replace her if she should retire exhausted.

One activity I am glad I undertook was to join the artists' group. The advantage of this was the small number of people involved, so one could lose the fear of always getting left behind. We examined many wonderful old buildings in our expeditions, and the time we spent drawing or painting them was very valuable. I didn't pretend to be any kind of an artist but what I found useful was being forced, when trying to draw something, to look at it properly – I am normally bad at this, being very unobservant, so it taught me a necessary lesson.

I found the long day outings rather self-defeating, because by the time I had arrived at the fourth site, I was completely unable to remember anything about the first. For example, the marvellous Aspendos amphitheatre wiped out the equally remarkable Side, which faded from my mind. Aspendos was the most perfect and complete Roman theatre, ideal for any theatrical event, including a modern pop festival. It could seat about 40,000, with acoustics to perfection – you could hear a pin drop. Pirge was the third stop, and I can only remember the remarkable entrance gate.

One did well to study the instructions for the next day's activities and where it said 'this excursion involves some uphill walking'

– beware. The day we went to Athens, which was both the worst and the best, the guides set off at a brisk pace and took us from the harbour side through an attractive little town to the wonderful auberges of the Crusaders. To linger a moment too long anywhere was to lose the group and then hunt despairingly for them among hundreds of other similar groups of different nationalities. Our assigned local German guide was very well informed and informative; in a former life she might have been a Gauleiter in a concentration camp as she raised her blue cap on the end of her umbrella high in the air, ordering us to keep up with her furious pace. At the base of the mountain we had to climb was a sort of Formula One racetrack, with quite a number of speeding cars tearing round it, seemingly intent on annihilating as many tourists as possible. Having negotiated this peril, one then had to rush up the hillside, desperately trying to keep the blue cap in sight. I could never have believed until I saw it the sheer size and majesty of the Acropolis; it has to be seen to be believed – photographs simply can't do it justice. We returned via the very interesting little museum and reached the bus in time for a head count. I will not forget how our guide said grimly to the driver: 'Only two missing! Drive on.'

Lycian tombs in the cliffs.

The highlight of the cruise for me was going to be Ephesus. Here I was extremely lucky, as Rosie had a friend who was a real live Sultana – wife of a Sultan – and who had promised to look after me on my arrival there. True to her word, she had done her stuff and a huge notice announced my personal guide with a taxi for the day. It was great luxury to visit Ephesus in such style, able to dawdle and look at anything I fancied with a knowledgeable guide to answer my many questions. The chief ornament of Ephesus had been the Temple of Diana built at the foot of a mountain and at the head of a marsh, a site less subject to earthquakes though it doubled the cost, causing diversion of waters; the amount of stone used almost exhausted the quarries in the country; between two and four hundred years were spent on the building, which was 425 feet in length, 200 in breadth and supported by 127 marble pillars, 70 feet high; when walking down what remains of the main street of the city, one could see the theatre, the gymnasium for girls – a sort of physiotherapy school – the library, and even the brothel. An underground passage had been found between the last two, which explained why the work done in the library by the philosophers took so long.

Some recent research just before my visit had revealed some noblemen's houses on the north side of the city; these were not yet open to the public but my privileged guide had access. The extent of mosaic work was quite astonishing; not only the entire floor but all the ceilings and walls – even the lavatories – were decorated in this manner; one ceiling was being lovingly restored with a brilliant coloured peacock, identifiable among many other birds. There was under floor central heating; the charcoal sent heat through the amazingly modern ducts penetrating the foundations and now plainly visible, illustrating what masters of plumbing the Romans were.

By the 10th century, the whole of this wonderful city was in ruins; it was the constant silting up of the harbour which caused the river to change its course, and gradually the port became useless and the town lost its prosperity. The large population, which would have produced the 40,000-strong audience for the theatres, disappeared, and the countryside now looked deserted. One can only imagine the rich finds which must be beneath the arid surface; some few earthquakes had no doubt helped the havoc wreaked upon this once elegant city with its marble streets and chariot wheel-ruts still clearly visible. Is it any wonder that the hordes of tourists with guides and buses and taxis and thousands of astonished citizens of this modern world congregate in such numbers and make it unbearable for the lone traveller? The country we bussed through had been rich in marble quarries, now one could only see fields of melons, cotton, corn, grapes and olive trees. Muscatel wine was much esteemed according to my notes. I finished the day dining with the Sultana, whose interesting domestic arrangements were quite unlike what I was expecting.

One other place I really wanted to see was the Corinth Canal, which was only finished in 1893. In the 6th century BC, the Corinthians had built a sort of railway – ships were loaded onto carts and dragged across the isthmus along a paved slipway – it was a laborious performance, so in AD 67 Emperor Nero had the idea of digging a canal across, using 6,000 prisoners of war; but he didn't live to complete it, so his diggings, that I had hoped to see, were destroyed in the building of the modern canal. It took us only 45 minutes to sail through at 4 am – surely the ghosts of those 6,000 looked on balefully at our progress.

As if time, corrosion, decay, volcanoes and earthquakes were not enough, the Greeks were always blowing things up by storing dynamite carelessly, even in such places as the Acropolis (no less) and Rhodes Palace.

At last we came to Istanbul, or Constantinople as I prefer. It is one of the most romantic and memorable places in the world – its domes and minarets with such historic names as Byzantium, the

Ruins on the Turkish island of Kekova.

Golden Horn, Haggia Sophia, the Bosphorus (where East meets West in reality) – the prize of the Ottoman Empire. We approached it at 5 am via the Sea of Marmara, passing the Gallipoli Peninsula where Churchill made his disastrous plan using the Royal Navy, which failed to break through the Dardanelles and during which we lost three battleships, with many more damaged by mines. It was of particular interest to me, as my father used to tell us of his experience during this battle (in 1915), when 'he was sunk three times in one day without getting his feet wet.'

Here as we landed I was met by more of Rosie's friends, this time a son of the Duke of Buccleuch, a charming young man. He and his Turkish girlfriend took me to see wonderful old gardens along the Bosphorus, the Cathedral Haggia Sofia, pointing out the exquisite ancient tiles in which he was an expert, and finally to Rosie and her garden, where she had planted her camellias. It was adjacent to her friends who lived in the very grand, modern Turkish house where we were going to have lunch. Camellias are magnificent flowering evergreens, the majority of which are as hardy as a laurel and will thrive in any good acid or neutral peaty soil. Their favourite site is in woodland with dappled shade, but

I enjoy a swim in Turkey...

...and then relax on the seafront - Kaldi, Turkey.

they can be happy and often flower more freely in full sun when planted against a south- or west-facing wall. Here, to do their best, they would need careful, regular watering and mulching. Rosie had chosen the perfect shady place against a wall and there seemed no reason for them not to flourish if she could arrange for their loving care.

Looking back to my contemporary diary of the voyage, I had written: 'Somehow not what I was expecting – I had imagined many earnest eggheads with perhaps a few frivolously inclined that I could lose myself among. I can't say I enjoyed every minute but I am glad I went, I have an indelible memory of incredible places I never could have imagined if I hadn't seen them'. So I continued to experiment on many other cruises on a nearly annual basis, always with some garden research in mind, being above all things an inquisitive plantsman.

RUSSIA –
THE GOLDEN
CIRCLE

My convent school education was supposed to have been followed by Oxford where my sister was already reading philology. But after staying in France for nearly a year, the second war broke out and I felt obliged to put off University until the war was over. I joined the Women's Royal Naval Service in the autumn of 1939, and it was a great many years before I found time and a core curriculum to my taste with the Open University – Oxford of course being out of the question by now. The inspiring subject I chose was 'The Age of Enlightenment' and I became fascinated by Catherine the Great. I always like to research everybody at source and I had wondered how I could get to Russia. It never occurred to me that I could explore this vast and rather secret country by boat. Catherine had a most dramatic life: she grew up as a minor German princess in the state of Stettin, and at only 14 years of age she was picked out by Empress Elizabeth I of Russia to be married to her son Peter, the next heir, who unfortunately was rather juvenile and less interested in his new bride Catherine than in playing with his toy soldiers. The Empress Elizabeth was the daughter of the brilliant Tsar of Russia, Peter the Great (1672–1725); she was known particularly for her vanity and it is said that when she died, there were 15,000 dresses left in her wardrobes.

Peter the Great was physically an enormous man – nearly seven feet tall – full of energy and enterprise; when only 17 he set out to travel through Western Europe studying all manner of modern technology in Germany, working as a carpenter in Holland, and when he got to England he studied every scientific subject, including astronomy at the Observatory in Greenwich, specialising in ship-building at Deptford Dockyard, where he lodged for several months with the eminent writer, John Evelyn; he was much helped by King William III of England, who hoped to encourage trade with Russia.

Peter then decided to open up Russia to the West from Saint Petersburg, where he invited the best engineers, craftsmen, architects, and shipbuilders to create his European 'Paradise', giving Russia access to the Baltic sea. He built a strong navy, reorganised his army to Western standards, and established the city of Saint Petersburg on the Neva River, moving his capital there from Moscow.

Catherine married Grand Duke Peter, heir to the Russian throne in 1745; she soon quarrelled with her husband and became notorious for her love affairs; shortly after his accession as Peter III in 1762, he was overthrown in a coup, supposedly orchestrated by Catherine, who was then made empress. A few days later Peter was murdered by Gregory Orlov, Catherine's lover, and others.

Catherine had a passion for English artists, above all for Charles Cameron, of whom she said in a letter to Voltaire: *'I am captivated by Cameron the architect, by birth a Jacobite, educated in Rome, he is known thanks to his work on ancient baths, he has a wonderful mind, afire with inspiration.'*

Catherine appointed him to build her famous bathhouse at Tsarskoye Selo near Saint Petersburg; he wasn't impressed by the local workmen so wrote home to Scotland and advertised for builders to carry out the work – 70 of them turned up. He took them all on and many of them settled in Russia and became well-known architects themselves.

Another passion of Catherine's was for plants – she was an avid gardener. During the Anglo-Russian *rapprochement* of 1793, she had sought a collection of garden plants from George III of England, but the war with revolutionary France delayed any action until 1795, when the king commanded Sir Joseph Banks (my hero, as some of my writings will reveal) to select plants from the Royal Botanic Gardens at Kew, of which he was the unofficial director. In all, 226 species of about 130 genera were sent by sea, under convoy, to Saint Petersburg for the gardens of the new Palace of Pavlovsk. Included was *Strelitzia reginae*, the Bird of Paradise flower, *pièce-de-resistance* and exotic, newly collected at the Cape of Good Hope – and named by Banks after Queen Charlotte, who had been a princess of Strelitz. In another letter from Catherine to Voltaire she had said:

> *'I love to distraction these gardens in the English style – their curving lines, the gentle slopes, the ponds, the lakes. My Anglomania predominates over my plantomania ...'*

Having been seduced into the luxury of cruise expeditions, I was thrilled to find that I could actually travel from Moscow to Saint Petersburg in a riverboat named *Alexi Surkov*. I felt this must have been meant for me, providing the chance of inspecting a most intimate and un-touristy part of Russia *en route*. Arriving at Saint Petersburg, I would hope to see where Catherine had built the special greenhouse for her new plants at Pavlovsk; something else that brought her to life for me – and that I particularly wanted to see – was the very special pavilion of Cameron's design at the nearby Palace of Tsarskoye Selo, dedicated to Catherine's favourite English pet greyhounds that she loved taking for walks. I hoped to find for myself the engraving on their tombstone which said:

> 'Here lies Zamira and the mourning graces ought to throw flowers on her grave. Like Tom her forefather and Lady her mother, she was constant in her loyalties and had only one failing, she was a little short tempered. The gods, witnesses of her faithfulness should have rewarded her for her loyalty with immortality.'

A three-hour flight from Gatwick to Moscow in August 1992 to join the cruise called 'The Golden Circle' was followed by arrival at the rather chaotic airport, where the very slow carousel allowed the cases from many different flights frequently to fall off into the middle. A bus to the ship took about an hour, where I found my cabin better than I expected, with two bunks and a big square porthole. After settling in, I went up to meet Ruth and Jimmy Joly – an ex-Wren friend and her husband who I had persuaded to come with me – and we celebrated our reunion with drinks and dinner.

An early start the next morning took us to Red Square and Cathedral Square, where the Cathedral of the Assumption held the thrones on which the tsars were crowned, and was decorated with the most superb paintings and priceless icons of Andrei Rublev (of whom more later), known to be the greatest of icon painters. The Cathedral of Saint Michael the Archangel, finished in 1509, was opposite the Cathedral of the Annunciation, with three golden domes dating from the 15th century; six more domes were added in the 16th century. Beyond was a small five-domed cathedral where lie 46 princes, tsars, and also Ivan the Terrible. We had an extremely good, articulate guide, Anna, who spoke perfect English, learnt at school, who said, 'A kind word is pleasant even to a cat' – no doubt a Russian saying with perhaps some hidden meaning? The tour continued, passing Lenin's tomb, Saint Basil's Cathedral, and the famous shop Gum, which alas had nothing much for sale.

Back to the boat for lunch – it seemed miles, along badly repaired roads, pavements, and occasional road works; many broken down Ladas (a primitive Russian make of car) lined the wayside, the drivers of which were only visible leaning into the bonnets as they struggled to make repairs. Few petrol stations and always with queues, as there was a great shortage of fuel and scant deliveries. I had tried to learn a little Russian before setting out, but even the alphabet defeated me, and try as I might to read the signposts as we approached them, I hardly had time. Another tour in the afternoon, and Anna pointed out a bridge which was decorated with pictures of Russian heroes – this marked the nearest point the Nazis had reached in 1944. On our way we passed the Victorian railway station, the Bolshoi Theatre (1824), which sadly we could not visit as we had to go the Russian Circus instead; we also saw the Novodevichy Convent, dating from the early 16th century, where Peter the Great imprisoned his sister.

The afternoon could easily have accommodated the Armoury, which I much regretted not seeing, or the Pushkin Gallery; instead we filled in time in Chekhov's house, followed by the panorama of the city, where hundreds of tabletop stalls sell Russian dolls and other tourist mementos – here I bought a fur hat for one of my grandsons – a really good deal at £5. Eventually to the Circus where we had a picnic supper. The entertainment consisted of terrible Russian clowns making worse Russian jokes (judging by faces in the audience), very sad bears, fierce, beautiful tigers (one man had a gun ready), very good horses with elegant ladies jumping on and off, a rather neat bronze tableau, and stunning acrobats with trampoline and trapezes – about 30 of them who leaped and swung and flew past our heads and high up in the roof, completing some of the most daring and terrifying catching and flying I have ever seen. Then back to the ship with a light refreshment on arrival.

Next day to Zagorsk. We were in the bus by 8.30 am and drove 45 miles along a frightful kind of motorway – I again tried to read the signposts but my Russian was hardly ever up to it – to view the Trinity Monastery founded in 1345 by Sergius of Radonezh; by the 16th century the monastery owned extensive lands and many serfs; the finest artists of mediaeval Russia painted here; and beautiful churches adorned with frescoes and icons were built within its walls. In the 15th century, the sculptor and architect Vasili Yermolin worked here, as did Andrei Rublev (1370–1430), and here much of his brilliant work is still to be found, including his 'Old Testament Trinity'. The Trinity Cathedral is one of the most perfect examples of early Moscow architecture, built as a kind of mausoleum over the grave of its founder, who was canonised in 1422. The iconostasis of the Trinity Cathedral is of great value, with the direct participation of Rublev and Danil Cherny. Ivan the Terrible ordered the construction of the Assumption Cathedral to add to the Monastery complex; its five outsized domes in blue and gold are a hymn to Russian faith and art.

After a picnic lunch, we returned to Moscow, where we visited the Metro under Anna's care. We followed her down fast moving escalators, and very deep to Pushkinskaya, got on and off trains at great speed, gazing at astonishingly decorated stations, stained glass, mosaic, paintings with no graffiti or dirt, and very smooth running trains with very polite people who offered us their seats. We came up for air at Mira Prospect (I think). There was then an optional hour to be spent in the Pushkin Gallery, which is the most elegant building full of well-lit rooms and finely hung Picassos, Impressionists, some 18th-century portraits, a particularly good collection and sadly not nearly enough time.

The captain's cocktail party took place after we sailed at 1730 hrs – this consisted of half a glass of Russian champagne (no seconds!) and a few speeches with everyone sitting down – no socialising at all. We then had dinner at 8 pm, after which I wrote ten post cards while the boat went through numerous locks.

The following few days were spent visiting Uglich, an historic little town easily seen from the river, and to which we walked. It is where Ivan the Terrible is supposed to have had his son Dmitri murdered. There are various theories about this mysterious death; one has it that Ivan killed Dmitri with his bare hands in a dispute as to whether Ivan had the right to bed his son's wife! The Church of Saint Demetrius on the Blood was built in 1690 and is of red and white stone which replaces an earlier wooden church; it has a cluster of five domes and the octagonal belfry rests on a square base, topped by a tent shaped spire. Some old 18th-century houses include the Voronin house, a two-storied building of wood in which the tiled stove still stands on the ground floor and is an unmatched piece of art. We listened to some Russian singing by four Orthodox priests, which I greatly enjoyed.

After another early start, this time for Yaroslavl, where the River Kotorosl enters the Volga, and there is a great confluence below the city which is said to be a thousand years old. In this city are ten churches dedicated to Saint Nicholas, who was the patron saint of commerce, very important to the people who lived by their river transport. Prince Yaroslav is supposed to have killed a bear here with a poleaxe, and legend has it that he founded a fortified town on the spot in the year 1010. It is, however, rather decrepit and has the usual pathetic empty shops. There was a concert of Russian folk music which went on forever, as these things tend to do.

Goritzy was the next stop, and once again we were surrounded by countless ancient churches, cathedrals, monasteries, some fortified, many of them of wood. These were the most interesting, being built from the nearby forests of the mature, slowly grown fir and pinewood trees, all planted very close together. When they were felled, no weapon other than an axe was used, no sawing which might let in air or damp, and only wooden nails were allowed. Some wooden churches had shingles or aspen tiles. All were lavishly decorated and had marvellous icons, many by the celebrated painter Dionysius and his sons.

There were occasional lectures on board about Russian history, and appropriately at this moment, a very good one on icons by Anna. There had been a very remarkable Novgorod School from the 12th century through to the 16th century, which was noted for its icon and mural painters. Andrei Rublev strongly influenced Dionysius (1440–1510), who was born into a family of painters and goldsmiths and is considered one of the greatest Russian icon painters of all time. He worked over his paintings and frescoes with his sons, who acted as his assistants and apprentices.

Occasionally we had some strange evening entertainment such as terrible local singers and equally untalented French dancers doing the Can-can and the Dance of the Cygnets, including one Frenchman of six foot four wearing a tutu. The food varied between delicious salads, rather good Siberian salmon, tough buffalo and some unidentifiable dishes.

The Grand Hall at Tsarskoye Selo south of St Petersburg.

At last Lake Ladoga came into sight and we joined the River Sver and Saint Petersburg at midnight. It was an early start the next morning for the thrilling Palaces of Tsarskoye Selo and Pavlovsk. It would take at least a week to do justice to seeing these marvellous historic buildings. Needless to say, there was very little time, and my efforts to find the remains of Catherine's mausoleum to her greyhounds ended in failure. There was no one who had heard of it other than to wave vaguely towards the garden. There also I failed to find any evidence of the old greenhouses specially built to house the collection of plants sent as the present from King George III and put together for her by Sir Joseph Banks.

The sequence of the saga of the king's present to Catherine is revealed in a series of fascinating letters from Sir Joseph to Sir James Burges, Under-Secretary of State. On May 6th, 1795 he says:

> '*In answer to your Favor of yesterday I have the honour to inform you that I have received the King's Command to Select from the Royal Botanic Garden at Kew as compleat [sic] a collection of Exotic Plants as can be possibly spared which His Majesty intends as a Present to the Grand Duchess of all the Russias.*
>
> '*His Majesty has moreover been pleased to direct that Plans and Elevations of the principle hothouses at Kew be immediately prepared by the Clerk of the Works in order that they may be sent with the Plants and also directed that one of his own Gardeners to proceed with them to St Petersburg and take charge of them during the voyage and give such information concerning the culture of them as the Grand Duchesses' Gardeners may have occasion to receive when they are carried on shore.*'

He encloses a catalogue of the plants for the grand duchess:

> '*I believe it is correct. The Stove plants do not run alphabetically because I could not refrain to start off with Strelitzia reginae – in the list I have kept the Botany Bay plants together which I hope you will approve.*'

He gives some instructions:

'The Great Cabin of the ship on which they are embarked must be wholly given up for their accommodation and a proper fireplace be fixed in it and fuel provided in case chilly nights during the passage render the precaution necessary. A fire may be kept up and a standing bed place for the gardener placed as near the plants as possible. The Proper time for the ship to sail is between 24th June and 24th July; before midsummer we are liable to frost in the nights in this climate and after the end of August winter approaches fast in the high latitude of St Petersburg.'

Banks picked George Noe, a young German who was foreman of the Royal Botanic Gardens at Kew, having been sent to Kew to finish his horticultural studies. Banks says:

'I thought myself lucky in obtaining him, because his German is precisely the same as that of Her Imperial Highness and he is sure therefore to be completely understood if ever she does him the honour to command from him any kind of explanation concerning his mission.'

Banks also wrote detailed instructions to Noe on how he was to care for the plants en route which told him that:

'All the plants had been double potted, a measure found by experience very useful in preserving the moisture of the soil.'

There is a long pause until the next letter to Sir James dated 1795, December 29th, from Soho Square, relates:

'Noe the Gardener who went to Russia is just now arrived after a passage of 11 weeks, by his account it appears that the success of his management was very good, he lost very few plants and when he carried his plants to Paulesski he found that only three of all those he brought had before been seen in Russia. The Grand Duchess received them with all possible honour, 15 coaches were sent to carry them from the water to the Palace and as they arrived there in the night the Garden was lighted up with lamps for the facility of unpacking them.

'The Grand Duchess was in the Garden by six the next morn and gave directions respecting them. Before noon Noe was sent for to the Palace and had the honour to exhibit the plans of the hothouses at Kew and the drawings of Plants he had been charged with to the Grand Duke and Duchess; at 2 they came to the Garden with 70 attendants. The Grand Duchess ordered the King of England's mark, 'G R' to be inscribed by Noe on every pot he had brought that they might not be confounded with her own and she every day spent an hour in learning the names of the Plants. When Her Imperial Highness removed to a Palace about 30 miles from it, she ordered Noe to attend with every plant that should flower and she with her own hand made a drawing of each.

'The most generous overtures were made to Noe if he would consent to enter her Service but he declined on account of his having had a recall sent to him from Wurtemburg where he says he is sure he never shall receive so much pay as was offered to him by the Grand Duchess. He received when he went away a handsome Gold Watch and 100 ducats as a present.'

It is interesting to read Noe's own letter in which he says:

> '*I was treated with a great deal of kindness both from the Grand Duke and Grand Duchess and they wanted very much to keep me, but I did not like the restriction the gardeners are under.*'

A wonderfully ornate ceramic stove - Tsarskoye Selo.

There is one more letter from which it is pertinent to quote, from Sir Joseph, who had spent a great deal of time and money on the whole performance. In 1796 he writes in exasperated tones to Sir James:

> '*Give me then my dear Sir your advice for if I am to do all, to write all, to direct all, and to pay all and no human being feels inclined to thank me I shall I fear in due time feel as sulky as a measly sow who has lost her scrubbing post.*'

A note at the end of the correspondence says:

> *'I received the whole of the money February 1799 being exactly three years after I paid it and no one has thanked me. JB.'*

Dragging myself back from the 18th century with difficulty, I noted that Tsarskoye Selo was simply as magical as its reputation. We learned that in 1941, the day the Germans invaded Russia, the curator started to take the treasures to safety and buried them all underground in Saint Petersburg. Eighty-five percent of objects were saved, including priceless curtains, chandeliers, china, paintings of Feodorovna and Peter the Great. Both palaces were wrecked on scorched earth policy and German spite, but now completely rebuilt from the original plans and no expense was spared. No doubt this accounted for there being nothing left of the old greenhouses.

Decorated parquet floor in the Tsarskoye Selo palace.

After this my diary describes a *'not very nice lunch at a gloomy hotel where we had blinis but no caviar! Accompanied by beautiful Russian dancing.'* Then a visit to Saint Isaac's Cathedral which had very fine mosaic and vast pillars of green malachite and stunning blue lapis lazuli – quite spectacular. There was a memorable concert that evening at the Smolny Institute, where the Russian male choir sang, making that extraordinary deep sound – like huge, angry, masculine bees – that only Russian choirs can produce.

The next day we visited the Hermitage, which was absolute bedlam. Very hot, millions of groups with yelling guides, and the huge lovely rooms, which contained the most beautiful Leonardos, Picassos, Impressionists, et cetera, and all the original collection made by Catherine, were all closed. One whole enormous wall by the staircase consisted of portraits of Russian military heroes, and where no portrait was available, the name would be under the empty frame. My diary finishes with: *'exhausted and disappointed to bed'*.

The next day, Yusupov's Palace was *en route* to the airport; it had been built by the French architect Vallen de la Motte at the end of the 18th century – five generations of Yusupovs lived there until the revolution of 1917 – they were one of the richest families of Russia. In December 1916, Rasputin was murdered in their basement, but although we carefully examined the actual spot where the crime occurred, we failed to find any of Rasputin's bloodstains. This was our last sight-seeing on the way to the airport and home to Gatwick.

THE INDIAN OCEAN

In case anyone was thinking of going with Jules Verne on an expedition, described as '*Wildflowers, Botany and Natural History amongst the little visited islands of the Indian Ocean*', they should not get overexcited about what they are going to see. I did and was rather disappointed. The blurb advertising this cruise said:

> '*Zanzibar with its Sultan's Palace, countless mosques and Arab buildings, steeped in legends of past riches, gleaned from gold, spices, ivory and the slave trade; Mayotte, one of the Comores Islands just north of Madagascar, surrounded by a 1500 km long coral reef, forming the largest lagoon in the world.*'

This was certainly seductive enough – the intriguingly named '*Nosy Be, known as the Tahiti of Madagascar, with untouched beaches and its holy crater lake*', merely added to the mystique. Seven days would be spent in the *Royal Star*, described as '*large enough to provide the facilities of a 4-star liner, but still small enough for the sophisticated, relaxed atmosphere of a large private yacht party*'. Lectures were promised on subjects such as natural history. The other seven days would be spent in the Flamingo Beach Hotel on Shanzu coast just north of Mombasa.

Let me say at once that, although I was somewhat mesmerised by the description, I did enjoy practically every minute of the fortnight; my disappointment lay in finding no snorkelling arranged (I had particularly asked about this), and no lectures.

We flew British Midland, rightly famed for its superb food, from Heathrow to Frankfurt, and from there African Safari Club Airline, owned by Karl Rudin of Basel in Switzerland, took us over. Rudin had had a somewhat chequered career building up his own airline; he started this as an airline operator in 1967 in Switzerland with the Globe Air Line, financed by billionaire R. Staechelin; after the crash of an aeroplane, irregularities were found during the investigation and Rudin had to disappear from the scene; he started up again in Kenya, a destination he knew from his airline background. With the Staechelin money, he soon acquired more hotels, and with his contacts of local authorities, among them President Kenyatta, and helped by his two sons, he soon became one of the tycoons of Kenya, now owning several more hotels, including the Flamingo Beach Hotel, where we were to stay, plus the *Royal Star*, our cruise ship. However, falling out with one of his sons, and his inability to work as a team, caused his downfall, which luckily only began to affect his clients the year after our holiday.

So our flight to Mombasa overnight arrived on time and minibuses took us straight to the hotel. This, as promised, was on the beach, but the thick, green weed growing visibly in the water prevented agreeable swimming, making the reef, in full view, inaccessible. I had written and rung up in advance several times to find out about what snorkelling (one of my passions) would be available from the hotel, how safe it was, and how much it would cost. No one at Jules Verne office had actually ever been to the hotel, so could not describe the set-up. But I was assured that boat parties of five or six people would be arranged every day, at about £5 per head – this, however, turned out not to be the case. I had also asked who the lecturer was to be and was told that no one knew or it was not yet decided.

Although the beach was disappointing, the swimming pool was superb – an island in the middle could be reached by bridges coming from either side, and fine coconut palms gave shade to the many sunbathers. The hotel itself was large and cool with open-plan reception rooms and large fans everywhere, also air conditioning, except during power cuts; it was functionally comfortable without frills, and the service reasonable without being enthusiastic. Not much was said about security, though we were warned not to wander along the beach visiting other hotels; we would be safer to take a taxi inland. Much play was made of greeting every local inhabitant with '*Jambo*', to show our friendly intentions – I got the feeling that we tourists were a rather necessary evil and that it would be their turn to be boss soon.

I found a message from a friend, Richard Wilson who lived in Kilifi Creek, inviting me to lunch the day after our arrival, so I rang him and accepted with pleasure; he gave me instructions how to find him and I set off in a taxi with a rather surly driver who seemed to know where we were going. We had to find a turning, left off the main road, signposted to their house, and Richard had told me 'if there was a problem just ask anyone' and they would all know him. Unfortunately the signpost never appeared and the country seemed deserted. I told the driver to find a petrol station but that didn't help either. I was beginning to feel alarmed, and not less so when the driver turned right off the road taking us in the opposite direction to where I thought we should be heading. Just as I began to despair at being lost in the middle of the African continent, a Land Rover drove by; I hailed the owner to ask if he knew Richard Wilson, and by a miracle it was him! I refrained from saying 'Doctor Livingstone, I presume', but it did seem this would have been extremely *à propos*. We followed him to his house and thankfully said goodbye to the taxi.

Richard and his wife and family lived in the most beautiful house in a divine setting – the Kilifi Creek being visible from both sides. After a well-earned drink and delicious lunch, we toured their estate in his new Land Rover. He specialised in cultivating and drying sisal, which covered many acres; he also farmed Friesian cattle which had been crossed with an Indian breed, resulting in them all being humped but also in their toleration of the heat. It was a lovely and most interesting day, giving me a welcome chance to see something of the African background. He kindly drove me back to my hotel to save any further catastrophe.

Keeping cool in the jungle.

After two days it was time to join the *Royal Star*; African Safari Club catered mostly for Germans, and this was the first voyage when a party of 20 or so English were included and 30 Americans, who caused a slight sensation by being described in the Mombasa press as '*American millionaires*', which they hotly denied. We were, however, surrounded by Germans, as is usual on foreign holidays – they always seem to be richer and outnumber all other nationalities. The ship was very well run by the Greek captain Vagelis Aravantinos. Our first introduction to him was soon after we sailed, when a very strict lifeboat drill was held; we found and put on our life jackets, lined up on deck as ordered, and hung about for some time before the captain came to inspect us – indeed it was so lifelike, we were afraid we might actually have to take to the boats. While waiting, the English and Americans all cracked rather bad jokes about whether it would be women and children saved first or the Greeks followed by the Germans! The crew were Filipinos, cheerful, honest and efficient. I had paid the enormous single room supplement and had a spacious three-berth cabin to myself. The ship rolled enjoyably; my steward brought my breakfast in the morning and the water was hot.

The *Royal Star* was a very nice-sized ship; there was a small swimming pool and plenty of room to sit and read or drink or play games on deck, though of course the shady seats or sun beds – as always seems to happen – were never available except to the Germans, in spite of rules which declared '*No Reservations*'. The nationalities seemed to keep together, and try as we might to fraternise with the Germans, they were very standoffish.

Wherever we arrived we had to anchor some distance from our destination, so a high degree of seamanship was called for and provided when the tenders ferried passengers from ship to shore in the quite strong swell of the vast Indian Ocean. The excursions cost between £20 and £30 per half-day, and we usually returned to the ship for meals.

Zanzibar was our first port of call and is a flat coral island populated mainly by Africans; its most important product is cloves, but it also exports copra, cinnamon, pepper, sugar and lemongrass. The old town of today was probably founded before the 16th century, and in the 19th century it became the central holding place for the East African slave trade.

European landowners built up their plantations on the mainland with the help of cheap and readily available slave labour. Dr

Livingstone was largely responsible for the ban on slave trading in 1873, and there was a small museum with many letters from him and exhibits of this period.

Other buildings worth a visit were the rather ugly Anglican Cathedral built with Dr Livingstone's help at the Old Slave Market, the fruit and vegetable market, the Arabic 'Old Stone Town', the Sultan's Palace and the Pharmacy, now under repair. Some of the private residences had enormous, very solid front doors, with huge brass knobs on them; I asked what these were for and was told that they protected the doors from stampeding elephants. The whole town was full of buildings in a sad state of crumbling, but efforts were being made to improve the condition of the better houses. During a minibus ride through the countryside of Zanzibar, spices, fruits and vegetables were to be seen growing in profusion, including jackfruit, papaya, the Zanzibar apple and 18 different types of banana, all cultivated for export. It was very hot in the brilliant sunshine.

In 1963, the Africans revolted against the sultans, and Zanzibar then joined Tanganyika to become the United People's Republic of Tanzania. The sultan is reputed to have fled, surprisingly to the safety of Plymouth in England.

The ship next called at Mayotte, one of the Comores Islands which, unlike the others when offered independence, chose to remain French and obtained the status of *Collectivité territoriale*, administered by a representative of the French government. It has in consequence excellent tarmac roads and other modern conveniences.

The island is completely surrounded by a coral reef, with only one safe entrance through which a pilot guided the ship. The inhabitants follow an age-old custom where all status derives from the grandness of their marriage; at 14, a boy leaves home and builds himself a small hut, which he covers in graffiti of various sorts to entice females to visit and finally marry him.

Mayotte is rich in wildlife of all kinds, little of which sadly there was time to explore. The exotic ylang-ylang, or perfume tree (*Cananga odorata*), is grown for its blossoms, which are boiled and distilled in a simple still, the trees weighted down to make harvesting easier. There are reputedly giant baobab trees in the south of the island.

The day after this was spent entirely at sea on passage to Madagascar. We disembarked at the island of Nosy Be and travelled in a minibus – in spite of the history and French influence here, the buses were all Japanese. The indigenous population are descendents of Malaysian and Polynesian peoples, immigrants from the Comores, Asia and Europe – they still preach a heathen religion, though there are some Christians and a few Muslims. We visited the well-named Hellville, in which was a small, round market building, surrounded by stalls mostly containing plastic buckets and other such items. The market itself was equally unappealing, with shrimps and meat covered in flies and very poor, rather menacing-looking local people; the children beg persistently, even climbing into the bus or pressing their faces against the windows. A tour round the island to visit sacred lakes full of sacred, but nonetheless aggressive-looking crocodiles was interesting; on the way were wonderful views of volcanoes, sea and island bays. The fertile country was covered in coffee and rice plantations, vanilla vines and bananas; there were stalls in the villages where finely embroidered tablecloths and shirts were for sale, plus vanilla, cloves and ylang-ylang (the scent plant) in little bottles. Many more begging children with lemurs on leads and chameleons demanded a dollar to have their photos taken; the lemurs looked overworked, bored and depressed.

On the return journey I spotted a small, yellow-flowered tree called *Colvillea racemosa*, which I had been looking out for, knowing that it flowered in November and was indigenous to Madagascar. I persuaded the bus driver to turn the bus round and take me back to photograph it and look at it properly. There were of course many tropical plants that one would expect, but I longed for a knowledgeable person to find me some of the other plants that only grow here.

Another day we visited an island called Shengu Mbili which looked very suitable for snorkelling – wonderful swimming in clear sea with promising-looking rocks, but alas no opportunity to plunge in.

That night on our return, the captain invited eight of us to dine with him and he told us he had served in the *Royal Star* for 12 years. He must have been asked every possible question many times but we managed to make him laugh once or twice. There was very large and delicious crayfish on the menu. Every evening after dinner there was some entertainment, usually complicated dancing of a remarkably high standard, particularly when it was the turn of the Filipino crew.

Now our week in the *Royal Star* was over, so back to Mombasa and the Flamingo Beach Hotel. Here we were offered some rather expensive tours, such as African Night, Bush Tour, Sinbad the Sailor, but I set about investigating the snorkelling prospects – with such coral reefs everywhere, there must be some chance of studying their secrets. I discovered the Serena Beach Hotel a stone's throw from the Flamingo Beach. It belonged to the Aga Khan and had considerable style; it had been built twenty years ago with much carved wood to give it an authentic Arab look, and there was a water lily pond in the centre of the open dining area with the most beautiful blue lilies in full flower. I found a representative of Abercrombie and Kent who was English and most helpful; in no time I had booked for the next day, driving south to Shimoni, a small fishing port, and sailing by dhow (local sailing boat) to take part in a snorkelling expedition masterminded by Bruce and Pippa, a South African couple who lived on Wasini Island. They had built their own 30-foot dhow and were in the process of producing another of 60 foot. They had also constructed their house from lumps of coral on the island cemented together, and as luck would have it, this day was the first time they had opened it to their guests, and a banquet was in preparation to celebrate. There were nine of us: seven Dutch, two Germans and me. It was a marvellous day with unlimited snorkelling; shoals of miraculously striped and multicoloured fish swimming unconcerned by us from several reefs in the famous Kisiti Marine National Park, to which we were escorted and looked after by local guides employed by Pippa on board the dhow. It was quite a long swim to the best viewing, but I was offered a life jacket which I wore in great comfort and security.

Part of the way the dhow motored, but later we progressed under sail, as in pre-history days. Putting up the sail or taking it down was no big deal, and the rolled sheet was attached to the boom with fibres freely available from the raffia palm grown everywhere. The banquet provided by Pippa herself, with the help of three local girls, was truly memorable and worthy of the Swahili Cordon Bleu Pippa had become. She served us the most delectable crab, caught that morning on the island and flavoured with all the spices of Arabia. There were salads and fruits of the region most beautifully presented in wide wooden bowls; on the table were carved teak fish with which we were instructed to bash the crab shells; and all washed down with unlimited, delicious South African wine.

Another place I found independently and which was well worth visiting was Bamburi Quarry Nature Trail. In 1971, agronomist René Haller began his rehabilitation of this vast, ugly quarry, which resulted in unmitigated success; it only covers two square kilometres but is at once not only a working organic farm, which produces everything from fish and crocodiles to coconuts and timber, but is also one of the main tourist attractions of the area. The taxi to it cost £5 and entrance another fiver, and it took about two hours to go round with a guide. He was a very articulate young man who showed me the crocodiles, which lived in the estuary and kept other predators away from the weaver birds, who make their very special nests safely above. The water from the estuary filters through the crocodile area to the rice growing field which distils it back to the fish hatcheries. There is a snake farm, a few hippos, and at feeding time about four o'clock, three delightful giraffes amble down from the wild to see what is going on. There were giant tortoises and many lizards, chameleons, monitors and iguanas, also some charming otters playing in clear water, surrounded by storks, cranes and pelicans.

The Indian Ocean holiday had been a great success, though my day of snorkelling, arranged by me, was certainly the most enjoyable part.

DOWN UNDER –
NEW ZEALAND
AND AUSTRALIA

I had often tried to imagine what New Zealand was like, fired by the many stories recounted by a neighbour in Cornwall who had inherited a large estate there with the most beautiful and historic garden. Many years ago, a scion of this family had eloped with the coachman's daughter to New Zealand and had become one OF the first settlers. After his first early struggles, the young emigrant started to build what became one of the biggest sheep and cattle stations in the North Island, and from his first modest homestead developed a fine colonial mansion with a garden that always reflected that of his old home in Cornwall. One day, when reading *The Times*, my eye was caught by an advertisement which described a trip round New Zealand by sea. 'Why not?' I thought, immediately envisaging Captain Cook, with my hero Sir Joseph Banks on board, sailing in HMS *Endeavour* to discover what they hoped would be the southern continent. I would follow their voyage of discovery as nearly as I could.

The ship was small, about 3,000 tons, just ten times the size of Cook's vessel. She was called MV *Oceanic Odyssey*, belonging to a firm I had never heard of, Noble Caledonia. Not only would I do my own pilgrimage, but the package promised visits to national forests, conservation areas and botanic gardens, as well as whaling stations, sites of flightless birds and other excitements. There would be time to visit the romantic vision which mirrored the Cornish garden created so many years before.

The outward flight (about 24 hours – that is dinner three times in a row) was direct to Auckland; I don't think much of stopovers, preferring to get it all over in one fell swoop. A short prowl round the city was arranged for us tourists on arrival, including the not particularly memorable Maritime Museum. We passed a volcanic crater which was worth a photograph, and the rather beautiful harbour as we joined the ship. The weather was cloudy and dull, but what lit up the place was a mass of brilliant scarlet flowers which came from hedges of *Metrosideros excelsa* still just in bloom and spreading away as far as the eye could see.

A Maori war canoe – Waitangi Treaty House.

The next day, a visit was arranged to the Waitangi Treaty House, where a magnificent war canoe awaited our inspection. It had taken three whole kauri trees to make, and 180 men to paddle. This wonderful species of pine is unique to New Zealand and grows to a phenomenal height, second only to the giant sequoias of California; its durable properties and the ease with which the timber could be worked made the kauri a much sought after commodity, and most of the forests were felled to satisfy the huge export markets of the 18th and 19th centuries; there are few of these monsters left, but Tane Mahuta (God of the Forest) is the largest living kauri at an estimated age of 2,000 years, a girth of 14 metres and a height of 51 metres, and is to be found in the Waipawa Forest, two minutes off the twin coast highway.

I had done a little research before taking off on this exciting venture, and made a few notes from Cook's log of the places he mentions, and which I might be able to see. I had also brought Banks' diary with me that covered this part of the voyage. The first place we would pass was called Young Nick's Head. This was so named as Cook redeemed his promise that 'of one gallon of rum to the man who should first discover it [land] by day, and two if by night; also that part of the coast of the said land should be named after him'. It was Nicholas Young, the surgeon's boy, who had the sharp eyes.

At a suitable moment I decided to go up to the bridge and cultivate a lowly member of the crew, who could advise me when we were likely to see Young Nick's Head and the various places I had pinpointed. This worked well and I discovered that we would pass the headland at about 4 am, although it would be pitch dark and we would be 40 miles or so from the land. I arranged for my new friend to telephone me in my cabin when the point was in sight. This he did and told me we could see the light flashing. I rushed to my porthole and there it was, far in the distance, but just as it must have seemed to Young Nick – without the flashing light of course – land ho! Honour was satisfied.

I had found out by this time that the *Oceanic Odyssey* was a splendid ship, and the other passengers seemed a very friendly lot. The weather had perked up, the food was good, the omens set fair for a successful trip.

That evening the captain was giving his cocktail party, so more introductions took place and afterwards we sat down to dinner with casual arrangements for seating – always a good sign on cruises. I found myself sitting next to a couple who knew friends of mine in Cornwall. Next day we arrived at the very scenic Bay of Islands, where swimming and snorkelling were available, although it was only just warm enough for such activities.

A whole day was spent meeting Maoris; there was no escape from their friendly greeting of rubbing noses and watching them do their Maori thing – can't describe! It was Rotorua next and the hot, bubbling, sulphur volcanic geysers – very impressive.

My friends arrived early next morning at Napier to take me to visit their beguiling garden which I wanted so much to see. I was not disappointed. It was filled with every variety of desirable plant and grown with the advantage of a more clement climate than that of Cornwall, and had been created with such long ago homesick yearning. Rushing back to join the ship before she sailed, I was able to admire the pretty, rolling, very green country, and to deplore the serried ranks of *Pinus radiata* planted for timber.

Finding myself once more on the bridge as we approached Cape Kidnappers, I asked if I might borrow their enormously magnifying binoculars. I wanted to see if the 'Haystack Rocks' mentioned by Cook in his log were visible, but although the 'tolerable high white cliffs' were just as he described, none of us could distinguish the rocks. By this time even the captain was interested in them, and to my grateful astonishment offered to take the ship in towards the coast to give us all a better view. There was one house on the cliff top and a huge rock in front of the cape – a splendid sight as the sun went down. We decided that the earthquake of 1930, or some other earth movement, must account for the absence of Captain Cook's Haystack Rocks. It was recounted that 3,000 hectares of new land were thrown up from the sea during this disaster.

'Windy' Wellington lived up to its name; it was also dull and dark, but warmed up later. It occupies the only gap in a chain of mountains 870 miles long and overlooks Cook Strait, which separate the North from the South Island. We took the cable-car from the maze of shops in Lambton Quay to visit the Botanic Gardens. Very little time there unfortunately and far too many begonias in the greenhouses. The famous Te Papa Museum was full of interest, but one really needed a week to do it justice.

After lunch the next treat was Saint Paul's wooden cathedral, built in 1870, where there was a plaque to John Cawte Beaglehole (1901–1971), the renowned historian who was born in Wellington. His lifework was the masterly Hakluyt Society edition of *The Journals of Captain James Cook on his Voyages of Discovery* (1955–1967), associated with which was his *The Endeavour Journal of Sir Joseph Banks* (1962).

The next day we sailed across to Picton on the South Island and I observed our arrival through the Picton Channel from the bridge – a rather dramatic, hilly range on either side with old whaling stations here and there. We were driven by bus for two and a half hours through vine-growing country – old glacier valleys and huge, dry riverbeds – then the National Beech Forest with plenty of southern beech trees (*Nothofagus*). I saw a New Zealand robin, much bigger than our variety, with a white breast and very tame. The weather all this time has not been up to much, and was now blowing a gale as we returned to the ship and sailed down Ships Cove towards the Cook Memorial, but there were to be no zodiacs (large motor rubber dinghies) ashore as it was too windy. Early the next day we were taken to join a huge fishing boat, from which we saw enormous whales, dolphins and seals. Another trip in the afternoon took us through rough seas where birds swarmed around us, particularly four species of albatross, including the largest, the wandering albatross. The fishing boat crew threw offal over the side and the obliging birds posed for us so close that you could almost touch them as they fought over this favourite delicacy. Dear little pintados and sooty petrels joined in the affray, having occasional fights – very enjoyable.

At Akaroa there was another very pretty, hilly view as we turned north, and an hour and a half bus ride took us to Christchurch where a tram ride trundled us round the city, showing us, among other things, the Victorian Gilbert Scott cathedral, which was so disastrously damaged by the recent earthquake; a flower festival showed off a plethora of marigolds in the Botanic Garden, where the greenhouses displayed the local mania for begonias. There were lovely trees, sequoias and swamp cypress (*taxodium*), which produce the most heavenly pale green leaves when their first spring growth appears. After lunch (not memorable) we went to the Antarctic Experience Exhibition, which was quite impressive, including a film – then back to the ship.

We paid a morning visit to some 'yellow-eyed' penguins and later to a disobliging royal albatross, which we observed from a hide sitting on its chick, without once showing it to us. It was an extra early start the next day specially to see blue penguins, which did not bother to turn up, but the very beautiful lagoon called Patterson Inlet near Stewart Island produced a few flightless birds called weka. Lots of parrots and parakeets flew around as we walked through the ancient forest with plenty of elegant *Podocarpus*. It was a pleasure to sit on deck in the warm sun afterwards, even though I missed a lecture.

Later that day the captain gathered us together to give us the bad news that we were being dogged by cyclone 'Frank' and must therefore sail straight on to Hobart in Tasmania, missing the fiords. This was especially bad news for me, as Captain Cook had also described West Cape, the most south-west point on the South Island:

> '*this bay I have named Dusky Bay ... The point of this bay where it bears SEBS* [south-east by south] *is very remarkable there being off it five high peaked rocks,*

standing up like four fingers and a thumb of a man's hand on which account I have named it Point Five Fingers ...'

I had particularly looked forward to this venue after missing out on the Haystack Rocks.

The weather had a menacing look and as I sat on deck, I did not care for the way the crew were nailing things down – it seemed a bad omen. We sailed north to Bluff to drop off some passengers, and then turned south, hoping not to meet 'Frank' on Friday – nemesis day – as he was reputedly gathering strength.

The management of Noble Caledonia now surprised me by asking if I could give my Cook/Banks lecture to the passengers on a day when we were at sea, so without any notes or slides – having come unprepared – I did my best, which included reading some of Cook's log and Banks' diary, which I had brought with me to study when we reached the salient points. My reward was to be any bottle of wine I chose from the ship's menu, but my audience was more generous and took me out to dinner when we reached Hobart.

The piece of ocean south of New Zealand is not a shipping lane; indeed it must be one of the loneliest and least frequented seascapes – with rolling grey waters and grey clouds from one horizon to the other – looking no doubt exactly the same 200 years ago. I was determined to sit on deck as much as possible and watch the empty seas, the threatening weather and observe the following albatrosses, which flew very high but seemed anxious to see us safely to our destination.

We now had a day or so in hand with Hobart, Tasmania to be our next port of call. I asked the captain if I would be able to get to Port Arthur (about 37 miles south-east of the state capital) from there, a small town I wanted to see, where the former convict settlement lay on the Tasman Peninsula. 'My dear girl,' he said, 'we will call in on our way!' He was the most obliging captain.

It was named after George Arthur, the Lieutenant Governor of Van Dieman's Land (Tasmania's original name); it started as a timber station in 1830, but is best known for its penal colony. It was the destination for the hardest of convicted British and Irish criminals, specialising in rebellious personalities, from other convict stations. The layout was symmetrical, a cross shape with exercise yards at each corner, the wings were each connected to the surveillance core of the prison, as well as the chapel in the centre hall. Here the 'separate prison system' signalled a shift from physical punishment to psychological. Many of the prisoners developed mental illness from the lack of light and sound; it was almost impossible to escape from this island prison; the surrounding waters were even rumoured to be shark infested. The mass graves on the Isle of the Dead was a tourist attraction, particularly as none of these was named. It was a sinister place.

As we were ahead of schedule, the captain decided to take us to the romantic and exciting Bathurst Channel, a narrow stretch of water that lies between Port Davey and Bathurst Harbour in south-west Tasmania. In 1772, Marion du Fresne, the French navigator, was the first to record the inlet when he arrived in the Bay of Islands. He was murdered by local aborigines with all 24 of his crew, and in the reprisals that followed 250 Maoris were massacred. After this unhappy episode a Huon pine timber trade flourished for a while, but when it ceased in the early 1900s, it was used as a whaling station. The area has never been populated but has had over time a number of reclusive inhabitants. Estuarine and introduced marine species have been studied there.

Now our pioneering captain was going to take us up the channel, and we would be the largest ship to come up since 1928 when an ex-naval sloop called HMS *Geranium* made the journey. After a rather cold barbecue on deck that evening, we made an overnight voyage up the inlet, which for some reason was a very bumpy ride. In the morning we climbed Mount Balmoral – very steep going –

and returned by 11.30 in time for lunch on deck.

The last few ports of call were Maria Island, from where we went by bus to Launceston, passing a wonderful lake and more beautiful mountains. All too soon we left for Devonport, the departure port for Melbourne, Australia. There was time to admire some elegant Victorian houses, then back to the ship for a farewell party with the captain. It had been a memorable cruise.

Although it was goodbye to Noble Caledonia, I had arranged an extra little jaunt as a final treat for me. The Australian National Maritime Museum had put forward the idea of building a full-scale museum replica of HM Bark *Endeavour* as the centrepiece of their floating collection. Many generous sponsors contributed to the project, including the Maritime Museum at Greenwich, and a great deal of interest had been generated during the six years it took to build her. Over 400,000 people had visited the ship shed to view the construction of the replica.

The primary concern had been to achieve historical authenticity and she was built to the same specifications as the original *Endeavour*. The main differences between the original and the replica were in the timber used, and in the modern paints, fastenings and fittings, as well as in the man-made materials for the sails and ropes. Instead of the traditional oak, elm and spruce, she was mainly constructed from Western Australian *jarrah* and other local hardwoods. The crew would sleep in hammocks slung from the deckheads of the lower deck, as Cook's crew did, but where Cook had over 90 people on board, the replica's working crew would be just 48.

After sea trials, she was commissioned on April 16th, 1994 as a fully manned operational sailing vessel. It was planned for her to leave Freemantle in October 1994 and sail south to Albany, then strike out across the bight for her new base in Sydney, visiting capital city ports along the way. I had read about this project and, thinking I might just be able to fit in a visit to her, I managed to communicate with her skipper, who invited me to come on board for a day sail if I could meet him in Sydney Harbour – this I was determined to do. What a thrill!

So when I left my cruise at Melbourne, I planned an extension which would take me by train (more interesting than air) to Sydney. My only friends in Melbourne, with whom I was staying, invited me to attend the Melbourne Cup – the great race in Australia – which happened to be taking place that day. I was afraid that my clothes would not be up to standard (knowing that this world-famous date must be something like Ascot), but as the heavens opened, gumboots and mackintoshes were more the order of the day. Norman and Dizzy also took me to visit the wonderful Botanic Garden where I could not believe the size of the gardenias, then to the Platypusary, which was the only place you could observe in pitch darkness these extraordinary creatures that make nests under the roots of trees, are covered in thick hair, have wide, flat, toothless beaks and webbed feet, yet are mammals, lay eggs and suckle their young. The males have hollow spurs on their ankles which carry venom, used as a defence protection.

The next day my kind friends dropped me at the station, from where I travelled for the first time in an Australian train. I had been invited to spend a night about halfway, at Albury, with some more friends, Tom and Olive Savige – Tom is a great expert on camellias, so their garden was a delight. Afterwards, another day of sightseeing, this time investigating another unique garden made in an old gold mine with a river running through it into a lake with an island, appropriately called 'The Diggings'; this had been made by and was the home of the best known dendrologist and plant collector in Australia, Ross Haytor. Then on to the amazing dam on the huge Murray river where the water flow is controlled by 14 exits, though only one was open and spraying with phenomenal force.

Continuing my journey, I had the pleasure of travelling all day through the magical Australian outback – at last I saw some wild kangaroos. I arrived in Sydney where lay the replica of *Endeavour* awaiting my historic day sail, and early in the morning I boarded her in perfect weather. By law she had to start her engine (which I could not approve of), but she manoeuvred under sail the magnificent Sydney Bridge, firing her mighty cannon with real cannonballs – the noise was unearthly – and she squeezed beneath the bridge again on our way out to sea between the North and South Heads, passing the memorable landing place of the first fleet of convicts. I sat on deck in great discomfort – but would not have missed it for the world – as the young crew practised hauling up and down of the massive mizzen, topsails, and mainsails. It was interesting to examine the cabins of Captain Cook and Joseph Banks (who travelled with his two pet greyhounds) and imagine the four years that they voyaged round the world together; and in spite of being at such close quarters (and according to their log and diary), not a recorded cross word between them. I shall not forget that day.

FROM PATAGONIA TO PANAMA

Escaping from England in January has always been a treat to anyone living in Cornwall, unless they are native to the county. I had only gone to live there of necessity (most people say 'lucky you', and there are indeed many advantages), having spent most of my life following His (and Her) Majesty's Fleet round the world (both my father and my husband having been officers in the Royal Navy). I am a sun worshiper, and after living in the West Country for over 50 years, what one remembers most is the remarkable rainfall. Wonderful for plants, and as a passionate gardener I am truly grateful on their behalf, but less so for me.

The county of Cornwall must be one of the few places where plants from almost anywhere in the world can grow enthusiastically, so it has always been an extra good excuse for me to travel to the homeland of every particular divine plant which I grow, and find out in what conditions it thrives in its native habitat.

Before I thought of cruising I pursued some of my pet plants by other means, sometimes joining groups with the International

Dendrology Society or the International Camellia Society, who often organised trips to study plants; I had also invented myself as a lecturer, and as such I arranged tours to America and Australia, but most of the travel was by air, train or bus, and it was the tedium of these that inspired me to take up sea travel instead. I had visited Belize, Guatemala, China, New Orleans, Cape Cod and California, among others; no one, I was told (at the period I am writing about), in their right senses travels by train in America, but I think they are missing something. As an example, on one of my journeys, while trying to get from California to Vancouver, I had booked a sleeper on Amtrak's Superliner, the *Coast Starlight* from San Francisco to Seattle; there must have been about 20 down-and-out passengers like me who were directed to catch a bus from the huge insalubrious bus depot, where we were greeted by a jokey little man who cheerfully explained that, as the train was four hours late, he would take us for a nice bus trip round San Francisco to pass the time. Meanwhile, he would only let us board the bus if we agreed to kiss him first, which, having no alternative, we all meekly did. I don't know if the other passengers were surprised by this or not – I certainly was; he regaled us with chat about the city until we arrived at the station and thankfully found the train awaiting us. My sleeper was on the upper deck of the train, which pleased me, and consisted of a long bunk with a rock hard pillow seemingly impregnated with tobacco and alcohol; opposite this – *en suite* as it were – was a tall thin door with minuscule shower and loo in a sort of cupboard.

The actual ride was quite spectacular, though all the places I had hoped to see by day were in darkness; the train takes you north through Sacramento, capital of California, and climbs the Cascade Range to about 4,800 feet, passing peaks up to 14,000 feet. To do this it does some remarkable hairpin bends and goes through no less than 22 tunnels, climbing 3,600 feet in 44 miles. It continues through Klamath Falls – where the scent of freshly cut timber pervades the air – to Eugene, the lumber capital of the US. Douglas firs cover the lower slopes and there are many clearings for felling. The whole journey is illuminated in October with the brilliant yellow of the big leaf maple. The train crosses two arms of the Columbia River, and from the steel bridge over the Willamette at Portland, the volcanic Mount Hood is visible at 11,235 feet. The line approaches Seattle along the Puget Sound (named after Vancouver's lieutenant) with the Olympic Mountains to the west. From Seattle one crosses quickly to Vancouver Island by fast ferry.

As my next expedition was going to be in South America it was time to investigate travelling there by sea. South America produces the most wonderful plants, many of which grow in England as if they were at home, and one such I had promised myself to visit in its native habitat was a favourite climber, the *Lapageria rosea*. I have grown it for many years in my cold greenhouse. Its Spanish plant collectors, Hipólito Ruiz and José Pavon, wrote about it in their *Flora Peruviana et Chilensis*, published in 1802, and I cannot improve upon their description of it, translated for me by a friend. It starts:

> *'There is no question whatever that the Copihue* [its local name] *is considered the most beautiful flower in our Flora. The intense red of its hanging flowers sparkle amid the dark leaves of the forest, making a proud adornment to our woods ... an elite member of the Liliaceae family, the genus of one species only was named after Napoleon's Empress Josephine, for her maiden name of Lapagerie, in compliment to her for her many services to botany; she greatly encouraged the cultivation of exotic plants by growing them herself in her garden at Malmaison near Paris ... Deep in the earth a rhizome extends horizontally ... sending out aerial shoots, the thickness of a feather quill, at first tender like asparagus which harden later ... but its search*

*for the sun saves it from extinction in the darkness
of the impenetrable rainforests; the free extreme end
is arched and makes circular movements in a clock-
wise direction, looking for a support. This phenomenal
growth is the cause of the twisting which allows the
shoot to attach itself to any suitable support and thus
continue upwards from left to right towards the sun.'*

How could one resist watching this remarkable plant behaviour?
I was lucky to have it at home in my conservatory where its huge,
beautiful, waxy, bell-like flowers develop singly from a tiny bud,
but later in the year they will hang in festoons from above. But I
longed to see it growing among the rainforests of Chile, so when
I saw that Noble Caledonia advertised a voyage from Ushuaia,
round Cape Horn, and up the whole west coast of South America,
finishing up via the Panama Canal, I decided that was exactly my
sort of cruise; the details given whetted my appetite even more and
I imagined there would be stops on the way where I might find
rainforests with the adventurous shoots of *Lapageria rosea*. I had
travelled with Noble Caledonia once before when following Captain Cook round New Zealand, and it had been a lovely ship and a
fascinating tour (see previous chapter).

My journey to join the *Caledonia Star* was not ideal – having to fly via New York/Buenos Aires/Ushuaia/Punta Arenas. A
compensation was meeting Sheila and Timmy, both from Ireland,
at New York airport, where we made friends trying to fill in immi-
gration forms – which were similar to doing an A level – only to
be told you had failed and must do it again. It was a lucky meeting
because we found we were kindred spirits and had the same sort of
sense of humour – an instant bond. Travelling as I do – mostly alone
– the people one meets are of great importance. To make real friends
on almost the first day is a luxury indeed. We still meet from time
to time and always keep in touch by sending cards from subsequent

travels; we haven't managed to share another cruise yet as Sheila loves to go to the Arctic – which would not suit me with my need for somewhere boiling hot – and Timmy is usually busy arranging musical festivals in the most unlikely places.

Timmy Reardon and I go shopping in a local market.

Buenos Aires is the capital city of Argentina and we settled into the Marriott Hotel for the two-day visit. It is situated on the broad Rio de la Plata, which immediately brought to mind the dramatic battle of the River Plate in 1941 during World War Two – our first and, for a long time, only victory. Early Spanish colonists in the 16th century named the city for the 'good winds' that brought them to port – now about ten million people live in the metropolitan area.

After a brief rest we were treated to a city tour where the Government House – painted bright pink – housed the famous balcony where Juan and Evita Perón addressed the adoring crowds. Our next stop was the Recoleta Cemetery – rather like a city of the dead with family tombs, mausoleums and monuments, crammed closely together, where one could easily get lost. We were led to Eva Perón's tomb which was covered in flowers. That evening we dined at La Parolaccia Restaurant down on the waterfront, and to add to our pleasure, a beautiful three-masted schooner lay at anchor close by.

Next day was devoted to the Isaac Fernández Blanco Museum, which included impressive exhibits of silverware, furniture, porcelains and paintings, and was followed by a visit to the famous La Boca residential area, built by Italian immigrants along the banks of the Riachuelo (a narrow waterway lined by meat packers and warehouses). Buenos Aires had first been settled in 1536 by Spanish conquistadors, but it was unsuccessful because of overwhelming Indian resistance; a siege forced them out, and in their haste to depart, they left their horses and cattle which were released to the Pampas; by the time they came back in 1580, the region was filled with wild cattle and horses – theirs for the taking. From the 400 head of cattle first introduced, the stock had grown to some 40 million, and by the 19th century Argentina had become the fifth most powerful and wealthy nation in the world because of the export of beef, leather and grains.

Returning to our hotel we were greeted by the dire news that *Caledonia Star* had been damaged by a severe storm with hurricane winds (gusting to over 110 knots); she had been struck by a rogue wave – something sailors dread. *En route* from the Falkland Islands to Tierra del Fuego (where she was due to pick us up) she had been faced with three giant waves approaching the starboard bow; she had managed to ride over the first one but the second was so close behind that she dived straight into the solid wall of water. In an instant, water was waist-deep inside the bridge, smashing

Torres del Paine national park in Chilean Patagonia. .

through four of the heavy strengthened windows, causing electrical shorts and knocking out most of the navigation and communication equipment in the attached radio room. In spite of the damage, she still had manual steering and good engines, but she would arrive a day late at Ushuaia and require considerable repairs.

Our expedition leader, Tom Ritchie, spent a hectic few hours reorganising our cruise schedule. The nearest shipyard in Patagonia was in Punta Arenas, Chile, so arrangements were made to sail her on there from Ushuaia. Meanwhile, we were flown to this southernmost city in the world, where accommodation was found for us in its two finest hotels which overlooked the Beagle Channel, and we were able to see our much battered ship sail by on her way to the refit.

Tierra del Fuego – 'land of fire' – got its name from Magellan when he sailed round the tip of South America in 1520 and observed many fires built by Indians along the coast. Now the name refers to the entire group of islands south of the Strait of Magellan (about 28,473 square miles), two thirds of which belong to Chile and the rest to Argentina. Colonisation by Argentina and Chile began in the late 1800s when gold was discovered, and there was dispute between these countries over the boundaries, eventually settled by intervention of the Pope!

Three buses were waiting for us next morning as we set off in brilliant sunshine (though by no means tropical heat) to explore the National Park. Snow-capped mountains rose directly from the sea, mixed in with fiords, glaciers and dense rainforests of southern beech (*Nothofagus*). You could tell the prevailing wind direction by the stunted growth of the trees resembling flattened umbrellas.

Magellan, Drake, Bougainville, Cook and Darwin had all been here. How surprised they would be to know that this is now the southern terminus of the Pan-American Highway, of which the northern terminus at Prudhoe Bay, Alaska is 11,000 miles away. Nearby we boarded a local catamaran for a scenic luncheon cruise; on the way we got close-up views of exposed rocks, where sea lions, shags, sheathbills and a few albatrosses floated or glided by. That night we dined at the Chez Manu restaurant, from where the view was snow-capped mountains, their peaks higher than 7,000 feet, forming the end extension of the Andes mountains.

At last the lengthy negotiations between the various government authorities were over and a charter flight was arranged to take us from Ushuaia to Puerto Natales in Chilean Patagonia; the nearest airport to where our ship now lay; what we didn't know until our arrival was that this was the first international flight ever to use this airport, and we were impressed to note how tight the landing was on the rather short runway. Puerto Natales, however, gave us access to Torres del Paine National Park, one of the most spectacular places in all South America. We were in for a long day, with a considerable mileage to cover, before we reached our ship.

The park covers about 450,000 acres, encompassing mountains, forests, rolling hills, grasslands, colourful lakes, rivers, lagoons and glaciers. I joined the excursion to visit a *pingüineras* (penguin sanctuary), and we walked on an easy sandy trail by the seaside to reach the breeding burrows – it was late in their season so we saw plenty of young ones. Tom pointed out wonderful birds, including Andean condors, black-necked swans, a black-chested buzzard eagle, some rheas, and numerous flamingos and ducks. We saw guanacos, small

American camelids which live in herds, a dominant male keeping a harem of a dozen or so females; it was time for a late lunch at the park restaurant, where we were greeted with Pisco Sours and delicious grilled salmon. It started to blow a gale as we set off once more on the very long last lap, and after several rest stops *en route* to Punta Arenas we found *Caledonia Star* awaiting us with a very welcome glass of champagne.

Pingüineras (penguins) sanctuary, Punta Arenas.

It was clear that the ship had seen better days – she was old and badly in need of redecoration; my cabin was dark and uninspiring, but at least I could now unpack. I heard that after this cruise they changed the name *Caledonia Star* to *Endeavour*!

The storm had caused me several disappointments; the first, that we had not been round Cape Horn, which I had really looked forward to, and now it seemed there would be no visit to the area I had hoped to find rainforests where *Lapageria rosea* would be climbing in search of the sun; and the temperature was still in the low forties Fahrenheit – much too cold for me. However the ship had not sunk and we had seen some unexpected remarkable sights. I had to give Tom and his staff full marks for how they changed the route at such short notice and still managed to show us so many exciting places. I joined Sheila and Timmy at the bar and we discussed the future itinerary.

The next morning we sailed through the Magellan Strait in highly changeable weather, coming out of its west end, where we were exposed for a short time to the Pacific Ocean. It was just as Magellan had seen it for the first time, when he completed his epic voyage, with no doubt better weather than we had been given that he named it for its calm pacific nature. We saw lots of albatrosses, giant petrels, brown skuas and terns, a few southern fur seals and sea lions. Some adventurous passengers had a go at kayaking, and Tom took others off to explore in zodiacs.

Every day was more breathtaking than the last, and after breakfast we reached the English Narrows, which are tricky to navigate because of a 90-degree turn between two small islands – it has to be passed at slack tide, and on the right is a small statue of the Virgin on Clio Island, ready to give a little divine assistance if needed. All was well and we continued for about an hour and a half to Seno Iceberg, enjoying the most dramatic scenery. Another ten miles or so and there was Iceberg Glacier – a vast retreating glacier made apparent by the smoothed-over, land-bound ice on both edges. Two groups of zodiacs carried us as close as they dared to the face of the glacier where we could hear ominous cracks and thunderous pops continuously; to add to the drama, quite large pieces of ice crashed off into the water from time to time. The colour of the exposed internal ice was a deep electric blue and nearby mountain slopes were covered in a dense growth of mosses which, when hit by the angle of sunlight, glowed a brilliant gold.

So far the weather had been fairly kind to us and now at last it was beginning to warm up. The naturalists on board pointed out Fuegian otters that they had never seen before. The drive was both beautiful and interesting as we entered the northern part of the Chilean Inland Passage; we were in the protected waters of Chiloé Island, and turned on an easterly course into Bahía Anna Pink; the channel became quite narrow and picturesque as we made our way between a number of large and small islands, including one called

Isla Fitz Roy (named for Robert Fitz Roy, Captain of HMS *Beagle*). The Patagonian cypress (genus *Fitzroya*) is also named after him, and is likely to live to an age of 3,000 years. We stopped by the Beagle Channel to walk along the water's edge and admire the trees and flowers. The small city of Castro is the capital of Chiloé Island, whose waterfront is lined with colourful wooden stilt houses called *palafitos*. There was a steep hill to climb to admire the amazing cathedral, which looked rather dilapidated from the outside with its roof covered in corrugated iron, but inside we were transfixed by its incredible beauty. The entire structure consisted of wood ornately carved; the pews were hand-made and intricately embellished on the ends; the columns were made of long, curved, narrow slats, and it had a raised hardwood floor. The fact that everything had settled and sagged through time rather added to its attraction.

The wooden cathedral in Castro, capital of Chiloé Island, is built from Patagonian cypress (genus Fitzroya).

Exposed once more to the Pacific Ocean, the weather was perfect and luck was with us when a blue whale appeared – this enormous creature presented us with marvellous views of its tall blow, the broad, flat rostrum (snout), and the long, smooth, blue-grey back – visible for a long time after the blow – and the tiny dorsal fin. Tom told us that it is supposed to be the largest animal ever to have existed on Earth. The greatest specimen known measured 109 feet and weighed 150 tons.

Caledonian Star reached the protected harbour of Puerto Montt before breakfast on another perfect morning and we boarded buses to tour the town and its environs, noticing the Germanic influence on its architecture. Driving through Rosales National Park gave us an incredibly clear view of Osorno Volcano. Later we took a walk round the vivid Emerald Lake; the great volcanoes were still in sight when we reached Lake Llanquihue – famous for its brilliant blue colour – and the third largest lake in South America. This must have been one of the most photogenic visits of the whole trip.

Once more back on board, we made for Valdivia, founded in 1552 by Pedro de Valdivia, Chile's third city. It has a turbulent history with insurrections, Mapuche invasions, pirates and the fight for independence. A wall was built round the city in the 17th century, with numerous coastal fortifications and castles; German colonists settled in the region in the 1850s and left their 'gingerbread' imprint on the buildings. The Fluvial Market gave us a close-up view of the local fruits, vegetables, seafood (shellfish, hard clams, razor clams, mussels, hake, robalo, salmon and seaweed), and handicrafts being sold by the banks of the river. Several very fat, rather tame sea lions were hanging about inside the market, waiting for handouts, and one very impressive bull named Panchito posed for photographs and gently took pieces of fish from the hands of a little boy tending the stall.

The next port of interest was Arica. Here the ship lay alongside and we walked into the port while admiring the Inca terns, roosting along the dock and perched on the hawsers mooring the ship. They are very special birds, slate-grey with bright red beaks and feet, and a long, flowing, white 'handlebar moustache'. We made the usual city tour, but here was the most memorable – unique in fact – Catedral de San Marcos de Arica. The previous cathedral had been destroyed by an earthquake in 1868, only one year after it had been completed – earthquakes are common along this tectonically-active coast – but this new cast iron cathedral in the neo-gothic style was designed and cast by Gustav Eiffel in France, and shipped as a flat-pack, in pieces, to Chile (was Eiffel the forerunner of IKEA?). It was erected between 1871 and 1875 and inaugurated in 1876, 13 years before the construction of Eiffel's better known tower in Paris.

Perhaps Eiffel sent many of his iron constructions pre-packed in those days – was it his own idea, I wonder? Or was it the far reaching effects of the Industrial Revolution with the introduction of iron in ship-building vessels, which could then be pre-fabricated in kit form and carried anywhere in the world? In 1875, Alfred Yarrow opened his own shipyard, Yarrow and Co, on the Thames, to build innovative vessels for the Royal and foreign navies, specialising in shallow-draft steam launches. His descendent Meriel Larken became obsessed by the *Yavari,* and spent 25 years researching the amazing story of how the President of Peru in 1861 commissioned two small gunboats (of which one was the *Yavari)* to be pre-fabricated on the Thames, and had them transported across the Atlantic and up the Andes to Lake Titicaca, 12,500 feet above sea level – the world's highest navigable waterway, where she (the *Yavari*) was reconstructed, and for over a century plied her trade up and down the lake. The pin-built order required six years to complete, in no less than 2,766 packages, with *'no portion of the foregoing materials to weigh more than 4 cwts'.* The parcels were carried mostly by mules, but where llamas took their place, a limit of 100 pounds was set; Meriel Larken, who took the trouble to travel the three-month, perilous journey from Arica in person, eventually describes the whole performance in her book *The Ship the Lady and the Lake,* and tells us – among many other wonderful details – that the llama, when overloaded, will refuse to move and spit contemptuously and with great accuracy. Meriel describes her determination to rescue the mouldering hulk of *Yavari,* which she found still on the lake in 1985, to buy and refit her and re-establish her – all of which she achieved.

The history of South America is long and complicated – there is no way I can even summarise the bloodthirsty Pre-Colombians – such great decapitators – the highly sophisticated cultures such as the Moche (c. 100 BC–700 AD), the Nazca of central Peru (c. 200 BC–600 AD), the Chimú (c. 900 AD until they were conquered by the Incas, who themselves lasted from about 1450 until the Spanish conquest in 1532). These cultures all left their palaces, temples and marvellous stonework, much of which we were destined to visit. Tom did his best to educate us with lectures prior to the next day tour.

The Peruvians seemed to have been the most murderous, and their warriors apparently battled each other, those vanquished being sacrificed. Their blood was put in a goblet and the goblet given to a god-like figure who drank it. All this was done in the service of a fanged god called 'The Decapitator'. In 1987, a rare un-plundered tomb was discovered, which contained the remains of the 'Warrior Priest' now known as the 'Lord of Sipán'. The items found in the tomb matched perfectly with the representation of the figure who is seen drinking the sacrificial blood. A whole day was spent in travelling by bus to view the site of this tomb and the remarkable riches in the Brüning Museum, but the ship had followed us up the coast and saved us considerable mileage.

The Nazca Lines, some thought to date back to 200 BC, were something else I really wanted to see and Noble Caledonia went overboard in arranging an amazing day for us. We had to start very early so our small planes could fly over the lines before the heat of the midday sun made the air unstable; we drove inland for an hour and a half through the Atacama Desert to reach the Nazca Plains, where the enormous scale drawings of animal and plant figures, lines and geometric shapes delineate the pampa and surrounding hills. Each aircraft took three passengers for a 45-minute flight, the pilot banking the aircraft over the figures so that passengers on both sides had a clear view. The figures include a tree, a flower, a killer whale, a monkey, a hummingbird, a condor, a pelican and a spider. The massive replicas are done in outline form with lines that never cross; the spider is 50 metres long and the monkey over 100 metres wide; the largest, the pelican is 285 metres. The geometric figures include straight lines that extend for many kilometres – rectangles, spirals, zigzags, radiating rays, and especially trapezoids. They are totally mysterious – their meaning has long been questioned. How could their draughtsmen have ever even seen them without aeroplanes? Some archaeologists think the figures are urgent pleas to the gods to send life-sustaining rains in periods of drought.

Lima (the nearby port is Callao), the capital of Peru, is another interesting place, planned by the famous Conquistador Francisco Pizarro in 1535, who founded and laid out the city on the banks of the shallow river Rimac. Next to the Viceroy's Palace is the cathedral built by Pizarro, but which was destroyed by an earthquake in 1746. The new (1805) cathedral has plastered adobe brick and cane walls, a wooden roof and massive wooden doors. We visited an extraordinary house, the Casa de Aliaga; Captain Jerónimo de Aliaga was one of 12 noblemen who came to Peru with Pizarro and built this house in which 17 generations of his family lived, right up to the present.

It was breathtaking – old Spanish tiles on the floors; wainscoting, panelling and ceilings of mahogany and other tropical hardwoods from Nicaragua and Panama in the 16th century; silk wall paper and crystal chandeliers; hand-carved hardwood chairs, some upholstered in silk brocade; ornately carved and inlaid furniture; religious paintings – all built round a central courtyard where an old *Ficus* (fig) tree rises higher than the house.

The Franciscan Monastery was once the training centre for missionaries whose parishes spread all round Spanish America. It is badly in need of repair – perhaps some arrangement could be made with the Gold Museum nearby, our last port of call, which looked as if it could easily afford to spare a few hundred or so ingots and bars.

We enjoyed some sea time on our way to Ecuador – now a nice 76–degree temperature. It is from this area that El Niño sends out his weather signals and influences much of the oceans. We went ashore to investigate Machalilla National Park, which consists mostly of tropical, dry scrub forest, but everywhere was covered in the luscious blue of morning glory vines. A curious tree called *Cecropia* lives here and accommodates colonies of aggressive ants, which in return keep their host tree free of epiphytic plants and other damaging insects.

The following day we crossed the equator with all that that involves – 'King Neptune' taking charge of the ship and members of the crew dressed as pirates having to kneel before the King and kiss his boots. The festivities and frivolities continued with a barbecue served on deck.

Our approach to Panama began with Las Islas Perlas, 'the Pearl Islands', which were rich in bird life as well as in pearls. Pelicans were the most prevalent, flying in long strings low over the water, plunge-diving for fish and soaring high over the islands in the company of frigate birds. We embarked in zodiacs to tour the mangrove forests, a group of trees, both the red and white species growing with their roots in salt water; green-backed herons and white ibis would perch high up in the white mangrove; there were also great-tailed grackles and blue-headed parrots flying noisily overhead; the most notable bird-sighting was of plumbeous kites, small birds of prey. We explored another island with a beautiful sandy beach backed by dense tropical vegetation, including a tree of the hibiscus family with large yellow flowers. The taller trees were covered in bromeliads and festooned with rope-like lianas hanging down from the branches.

Next day was to be the Panama Canal, and we were lucky to be promised a daytime transit. The construction of a waterway from the Atlantic to the Pacific across Central America had been envisaged since Spanish Colonial times, but the French attempt did not begin until 1880. This was an expensive failure when the French, hoping to economise by using local labour, and not bothering to spend money on health precautions, lost nearly 20,000 men to disease – mostly malaria and yellow fever – and gave up after 20 years. Following a great deal of argument, the United States bought the rights and interests of the French company and signed a treaty between the US and Panama in 1903, which gave them the right to operate the canal in perpetuity. Construction actually began in 1909 after years of surveys and disease control. The eradication of malaria and yellow fever was a notable achievement – without it there would have been no canal. A lock canal was decided upon, which involved digging through the Continental Divide (here only 312 feet in elevation) and building what were at the time the largest earthen dam, the largest man-made lake, the largest locks and the largest gates ever constructed. The first transit occurred on 15th August 1914.

Paradoxically, the canal – which is 51 miles long – runs from south-east to north-west, so the Pacific entrance at Balboa is actually east of the Atlantic exit at Colón.

Early in the morning we awoke to find ourselves at Balboa, surrounded by ships of all sizes awaiting their turn for their transit. Our pilot, who would provide the commentary, came aboard and we passed under the Bridge of the Americas, which carries the Pan-American Highway (about halfway to Alaska by now). A group of line-handlers connected steel cables to four 'mules' – electric-powered railroad engines – fore and aft, port and starboard, to help pull us through to reach the Gatun Lake by lunchtime. Birds were everywhere, laughing gulls with black heads, magnificent frigate birds and black vultures; two species of migrating hawks joined together in immense flocks soaring above us; there were also some keel-billed toucans with bright yellow bibs; even a few howler monkeys could be spotted in the distant trees. Late in the afternoon we entered the Gatun locks to complete our transit of the canal.

That night was the captain's farewell cocktail party and dinner. It had been a most successful trip in spite of the early disaster; we felt astonished that it was so painless and enjoyable to follow the paths of such historic pioneers as Pizarro, Balboa, Magellan, Darwin, and Fitz Roy. We had had our fill of subarctic scrub, rainforests, deserts, glaciers and volcanoes in the comparative comfort of *Caledonia Star*, and were grateful to her for always being there to pick us up after our long excursions by bus. Timmy and Sheila and I said our farewells, but we were certainly going to meet again.

DOWN THE YANGTZE

The International Camellia Society meet in a different country each year; I had been with them to New Orleans once, but now they were going to China. This is a country I had longed to visit but the journey seemed such a marathon; now, however, I was spurred on by the knowledge that a great friend of mine, aged 94, was also going (on her way to visit her great-grand children in Australia); this was typical of Vi Lort Phillips, an indomitable traveller – even though she was waiting to get the necessary permission of her doctor she was determined to go. So if I was not too late to book a cruise down the Yangtze Kiang – where the doomed Gorges of the river were due to be flooded in a few months time – I would then join up with Vi.

It was Vi who had originally taken me under her wing and made me join both the International Camellia Society and the International Dendrology Society. She promised to introduce me to the most interesting members of both and make sure I sat next to them at their social functions. She had been President of the Camellia

Society for many years and knew everything and everybody and was a great help to me – a mere beginner. She lived in Jersey, where she had helped Gerald Durrell design the lovely garden round his zoo. When I visited the zoo with her, she seemed to know all the marmosets by name and they made acknowledging noises of greeting in return. Vi made a habit of inspecting zoos wherever camellia tours took her, and I remember the New Orleans visit where there was a zoo she was particularly interested in, and it had been closed for the only day we could be there. However, when I managed to get hold of the top zoo manager, he kindly arranged to show us round when he heard who wanted to see it. I was much impressed by the enormous python in the reptile house, which had curled its immense body round a huge pile of eggs – some of which were beginning to hatch.

All my plans for the expedition to China fell into place and I met my guide, Yankee Yang, after an all-night flight to Beijing, followed by a three-hour wait for a connecting flight to Shanghai. I discovered that your guide in China is a sort of nanny, but one with very limited English. Conversation has to be in previously composed phrases – communication beyond these is difficult. She was able to tell me that there was no dinner in my hotel so I must go out to some place she had arranged for 6 pm. I was resigned to do everything she said as I had no alternative. I dined alone in state in a funny little restaurant in Chao Bao Road, where she had already decided what I was going to eat. I tried asking for wine but they only understood beer – so I gave up and had tea. I approached my dinner gingerly as I couldn't seem to recognise any of the dishes; however, it only cost US $4. I gathered that we were now to be entertained by Chinese acrobats in the Shanghai Grand Theatre. Even in my fairly exhausted state I could not help being astonished by the amazing feats; one of their most enthusiastic efforts was to climb one on top of each other until there were about 15 of them, with the top athlete standing on the others, waving some trophy. I managed with difficulty to persuade my guide eventually to take me back to my hotel.

Before joining my cruise I discovered that I had a day's sightseeing in Shanghai, and a new guide called Eleanor would collect me first thing next day to take me to visit the Yuyuan Garden. It was surrounded by very old impressive walls, but had no very memorable plants that I could recognise. The next excitement was tea tasting, and as the only customer in a very large shop, I sat down before a huge array of different teas. The lady showing it all off poured a kettle of not quite boiling water randomly all over a great many cups of different teas for me to taste; I tried black green tea, which was very bitter; a jasmine tea, which as I watched turned the blue dragon decorating the cup bright yellow; there was another variety which had a fat little bud which came out in the cup when you added the water; the best was another so-called jasmine with a red flower, which was very refreshing, warming and delicious, so I bought a small packet of it for US $14. I inquired about its origins and was told it came from a red clover flower from Tibet. So much for China tea, which actually is made from the camellia leaf – *Camellia sinensis*, the tea plant, which is grown all over the hills in this part of China – I was looking forward to seeing it 'in the flesh' as we drove around.

Lunch was at a not very nice café and Eleanor suddenly disappeared; I was quite alarmed as I had no idea where I was. At last she re-appeared and I insisted on having a rest before further sightseeing. We then visited the Bund and the Oriental Pearl Tower – in heavy rain by this time, but both very memorable.

The Bund is a waterfront area in central Shanghai. It lies north of the old walled city and was initially a British settlement. Magnificent commercial buildings in the Beaux-Arts style sprang up around the turn of the 20th century and the Bund developed into a major financial centre for the whole of south-east Asia.

The Oriental Pearl TV Tower is surrounded by Yangpu Bridge

in the north-east and Nanpu Bridge in the south-west and creates a picture of two dragons playing with pearls. The scene is a photographic jewel and attracts thousands of visitors all year round. These same visitors can travel up and down the tower between the spheres in double-decker elevators that can hold 50 people, at the rate of seven metres per second.

Eleanor eventually restored me to my hotel with instructions to be ready for an early start next day, when she would take me to the airport from where I was to fly, apparently to Chongqing. My guides never let me even see my airline ticket until I was safely on the plane. I was, in fact, treated entirely like a well-labelled parcel. When I got to my seat, I discovered where I was going and that there I was supposed to pick up my river cruise.

On arrival, the next guide was able to explain that for some mysterious reason the river was not deep enough to accommodate the five-star boat because there was not enough water in the great Yangtze Kiang. I would have to wait about six hours until a bus would take me to Fengdu, where hopefully the boat would be waiting. My guide then drove me round the city, which was a most depressing, gloomy-looking place. We visited the Museum of The Three Gorges, which was fascinating and explained with many illustrations and models all about the dam. It was going to be in place and operational by June 2003 – that very same year, in only a few months time. The level of the river would rise five meters per hour from 70 metres to 136 metres in 15 days approximately, where it would stay until 2009 and by then would reach 170 metres. All the inhabitants of the area were being forced out of their houses whether they liked it or not, and they were to be re-housed in dwellings with modern equipment such as lavatories, cookers and such items. One gathered that they were horrified at the prospect.

The Chinese are very good at occupying their tourists in profitable (to them) ways; the silk factory with a restaurant attached was a case in point. Having been shown the entire process of silk making, from the mulberry to the silk duvet, and been given plenty of time and a personal guide to examine every beautiful silk garment in the shop – naturally I could not resist buying a most elegant jacket – I was then taken to the restaurant, where once more my menu was chosen for me. I gazed at the unidentifiable prawn-like insects on my plate and suddenly remembered where I had seen them before: the silk worms, of course, feeding on mulberries! No doubt these were the old-age pensioners, no longer useful in the silk factory, but which could earn their pensions by becoming a Chinese sandwich.

After lunch we drove along the river, which was certainly very low; I was taken to a small, dilapidated, no-star and no shock absorber bus, which was to transport me down river to Fengdu, where hopefully my boat awaited. There were in fact two buses, and my guide tried to make me put my suitcase in the other one, but here I strongly resisted and this time I won. I was astonished at first to find myself the only passenger; gradually the bus filled up with all Chinese and a lot of children who all kept getting off again; the bus showed no signs of going anywhere or even having a driver. My guide had by now completely disappeared and I began to wonder if I was in the right vehicle. In desperation as time went by and it got really full, I got to my feet and asked loudly if anyone spoke English and where the bus was going? To my intense relief, a young Chinese man answered me in excellent American and reassured me of the bus's destination. He later told me he was the administrator of 'Front Desk', an employment agency in Wuhan, and was taking a group outing for his firm. According to him, Wuhan was China's ninth largest city and was getting bigger and bigger, but was very under-populated – hence it was called 'Ghost Town' – the government was trying to push the policy of urbanisation. We eventually arrived at Fengdu at about 10 pm that night, and I was shown my cabin by a very bossy man; I complained to him that the lock on my cabin was faulty and that there was no hot water, before also finding that there was nothing to eat and the bar was closed. I noted in my diary, '*I shall soon be thin*'.

With the problems of my cabin lock and the hot water in the shower room eventually sorted out, next morning I joined the other passengers going ashore to see the ghost town of Wuhan. We could examine the dilapidated remains of the houses emptied of their occupants along the river bank. At least I was seeing a few unexpected parts of China with all these delays.

Yangtze riverside houses abandoned to make way for the hydro-electric dam.

Back to the boat for lunch, and soon after we sailed and began the exciting cruise. The fast flowing river narrowed as we progressed, and the next morning we raced through the sensational Three Gorges in the day. I occupied myself trying to photograph the narrow towpath, cut in the sheer perpendicular rocks about 200 feet above the surface of the water. The river varied between 50 and 100 feet wide between the massive rocky gorges hundreds of feet high.

I could not help thinking of Robert Fortune (1813–1880) who

described in his book, *Three Years Wandering in China* (which I had brought with me), how these pathways were used by the trackers whose job it was to haul the boats upstream against the ferocious currents. He recounts:

> '*Every now and then we came to some rapids, which took us hours to get over, notwithstanding that fifteen men, with arm-thick plaited bamboo ropes fastened to the mast of our boat were tracking along the shore and five or six more were poling with long bamboos; nothing shows so much as this the indefatigable perseverance of the Chinese, when looking upon a river such as this one would think it quite impossible to navigate.*'

Plainly visible and parallel with these narrow tracks was another pathway higher up the vertical mountain, along which the imperial court officials and rich merchants would have travelled, carried in bulky sedan chairs by coolies. This was the only road-path connecting the provinces of Fengjie and Daxi, and these ancient pathways – only a few feet wide – were built with such basic tools as hammers, chisels and awls. It is difficult to imagine how the coolies kept their footing and could still move at the required speed. All these paths will vanish when the river is flooded.

At the entrance to the third Gorge we disembarked into small wooden boats and were towed by modern-day trackers, who punted, pushed, towed or kedged us up the Shenlong River (a tributary of the Yangtze), with eight or so young men to a boat and 15 passengers in each. They were bare-legged, often up to their thighs in mud and water, using plaited bamboo ropes and long bamboos with hooks while urging each other on with a powerful age-old shanty or war-song known as the Wei Hi chorus, which must have been passed down from their ancestors.

That night, the captain gave a reception followed by dinner on

*Punted, pushed, towed and kedged up the Third Gorge in a
way that cannot have changed much over the centuries.*

board. I found I was the only English passenger and made friends with a very nice Frenchman and his Indian wife; there was an interesting Mexican couple as well as an American mother and grown-up son. The next day the river became wider and the mountains were not so high. We were approaching the dam, which we would explore the following day.

Three Gorges dam is the world's largest
hydro-electric construction.

We left the ship at 8 am on our way to the airport at Yichang. I had spent a tortured night being frightfully sick, but in spite of my enfeebled state I felt well enough to pack and proceed. Heaven knows what I had eaten. We stopped at Maoping to inspect the huge dam, which was far from finished but very interesting. This vast enterprise was China's Three Gorges Dam, the world's largest hydroelectric dam based on generating capacity. It is 1.3 miles wide, over 600 feet in height, and has a reservoir that stretches 405 square miles. The latter helps control the flooding on the Yangtze River and allows 6,000-ton freighters to sail into the interior of China six months of the year. The 32 main turbines are capable of generating as much electricity as 18 nuclear power stations. It cost US $59 billion and took 15 years to build. It was the largest project in China's history since the Great Wall. In order for the dam to exist, over 100 towns had to be submerged, resulting in the relocation of 1.3 million people.

After this mind-boggling experience, it was 30 miles on to the airport, where the flight to Shanghai was delayed three hours. On arrival I joined the ICS tour, who had already had dinner, but was glad to go early to bed.

Perhaps I should finish my experiences of China by describing an adventure that happened to Robert Fortune (though it was not exactly a cruise), and I quote from the blurb on his book published in the middle of the 19th century. He was a novice traveller whose only language was English, but he survived robbery, assault, fever, a typhoon and an attack by pirates during the course of his travels, yet still managed to fill his Wardian cases (small glass houses for conveying plants) with *'the most beautiful plants of northern China'*.

As Botanical Collector to the Horticultural Society of London he had been travelling down the River Min and now wanted to get back to Chusan – the only means of travel was by boat. Knowing how much the natives disliked foreigners, he had been pleasantly surprised to find himself welcomed on board what was to be a fleet of junks, as he describes: *'about 170 sail – all like ourselves, loaded with wood and ready to start for the northern ports of Ningpo and Chapoo'*. The captain of the junk enquired whether Fortune had his gun and pistols in proper order, with plenty of powder and ball; he and his sailors were very uneasy about the voyage, expecting attacks by *Jan-dous* (pirates); the Chinese were forbidden to carry arms, which accounts for Fortune's welcome on board. Fortune laughed and undertook to beat off any pirates – not taking them very seriously. They sailed early next day, but late in the afternoon the captain and pilot came hurriedly to Fortune to report a number of *Jan-dous* right ahead, '*lying in wait for us*'. He recounts:

> '*By the aid of a small pocket telescope, I could see as the nearest junk approached that her deck was crowded with men; I had no longer any doubts regarding her intentions; I knew perfectly well if we were taken by the pirates I had not the slightest chance of escape – the first thing they would do would be to knock me on the head and throw me overboard. The scene around me was now a strange one …*'

He tells of how the captain, pilot and crew were taking up the floor-boards and hiding their money and valuables; baskets of stones were brought up from the hold, which were to be used instead of firearms, and they all now, including his servants, changed into ragged clothes so as not to appear to be worth kidnapping. He continues:

> '*The nearest pirate was now within two or three hundred yards of us and putting his helm down gave us a broadside from her guns; everyman on board now ran below except two who were at the helm. I expected every moment that these would also leave their posts – then we would be easy prey to the pirates. 'My gun is nearer you than those of the Jan-dous,' said I to the two men, 'and if you move from the helm, depend upon it I will shoot you'. The poor fellows kept their posts; we had every stitch of sail set and a fair wind and were going through the water at a fair rate of seven or eight miles an hour. The shot from the pirates fell considerably short of us; I was therefore enabled to form an opinion of the range and power of their guns, which was of some use to me. Assistance from our*

cowardly crew was quite out of the question for there was not a man among them brave enough to use the stones which had been brought on deck; our pursuers were gaining rapidly upon us; again the nearest pirate fired upon us – the shot this time fell just under our stern. I still remained quiet, as I had determined not to fire a single shot until I was quite certain my gun would take effect. The third broadside came whizzing over our heads and through the sails without however wounding either myself or the helmsmen. The pirates now seemed quite sure of their prize and came down upon us hooting and yelling like demons, and at the same time loading their guns, evidently determined not to spare their shot. This was a moment of intense interest. The plan which I had formed from the first was now to be put to the proof; and if the pirates were not the cowards which I believed them to be, nothing could save us from falling into their hands. Their fearful yells seem to be ringing in my ears even now, after this lapse of time, and when I am on the other side of the globe.

'The nearest junk was now within thirty yards of ours; their guns were loaded and I knew that the next discharge would completely rake our decks. 'Now,' I said to our helmsmen, 'keep your eyes fixed on me and the moment you see me fall flat on the deck do the same or you will be shot.' I knew that the pirate who was now on our stern could not bring his guns to bear upon us without putting his helm down and bringing his gangway at right angles to our stern as his guns were fired from the gangway. I therefore kept a sharp eye on his helmsman, and the moment I saw him putting the helm down I ordered our steersman to fall flat on their

*faces behind some wood and at the same moment did
so myself. We had scarcely done so when bang! bang!
went their guns and the shot came whizzing close over
us, splintering the wood in all directions. Fortunately
none of us was struck. 'Now, mandarin, now! They
are quite close enough!' cried my companions, who
did not wish to have another broadside like the last;
I being of the same opinion raised myself above the
high stern of our junk; and while the pirates were not
more than twenty yards from us, hooting and yelling, I
raked their decks, fore and aft with shot and ball from
my double-barrelled shotgun.*

*'Had a thunder bolt fallen amongst them, they could
not have been more surprised. Doubtless many were
wounded and probably some killed. At all events, the
whole of the crew, not fewer than forty or fifty men,
who a moment before crowded the deck, disappeared
in a marvellous manner; sheltering themselves behind
the bulwarks or lying flat on their faces. They were so
completely taken by surprise that their junk was left
without a helmsman; her sails flapped in the wind; and
as we were still carrying all sail and keeping on our
right course, they were soon left a considerable distance behind.'*

As the experience of *Le Ponant* in a later chapter points out, there
is some relevance in Fortune's story to the present threats by
pirates in the Indian Ocean – perhaps his tactics should be studied
by those in charge when it comes to sailing off the Somali coast.

Joining up with the ICS I found Vi in very high spirits; there
were several hundred members from many different countries and
it was a pleasure to renew acquaintance with some I had not seen
since the previous tour. About eight huge buses transported us from

one camellia collection or meeting place to another, and wherever we went Vi was always the star. The Chinese revere old people, and consider they bring good luck; sometimes, when Vi was in a wheel-chair, another friend of hers or I would push her while she waved happily in a splendidly rather 'Queen-Motherly' royal manner to the admiring crowds, and smile to the many children who were brought up to touch her skirt or hand.

Vi Lort Phillips – the indomitable traveller.

We stayed in very good hotels for the duration of the tour but always had difficulty in being served with wine – beer seemed to be the only drink they understood. However, eventually we found a variety of white wine called 'Dynasty', and fairly nasty it was. At the end of the tour, Vi went off to visit her great-grandchildren in Australia (as one would expect, Vi lived to be over a hundred). I returned to the UK with the rest of the group.

EAST AFRICA –
A LETTER FROM DAR

One often hears of people who have outrageous strokes of luck, such as unexpected legacies, winning the lottery or something equally unlikely, but it does not usually happen to oneself – well not to me anyway. Imagine my astonishment when a friend, Vanessa, who lives in London, rang me and said: 'You are always moaning about being cold – drop everything and join this cruise, which, because of some crisis, has not got enough passengers for her next voyage in the Indian Ocean, and rather than cancel the whole thing, tickets for two weeks are being offered at £1,200 instead of the real price, which is £9,000!' Well naturally I dropped everything and found myself winging my way to Nairobi, from where I had to find Dar es Salaam (if you are in the know, apparently just called 'Dar'!), where I would find the wonderful ship SS *Hebridean Spirit* waiting for me. Twelve of us had been included by Vanessa in this offer, and I cannot describe this thrilling and unexpected treat better than by quoting my 'thank you' letter to her after my return.

*On arrival in every harbour we were greeted
by floating salesmen.*

My dear Vanessa,

*Thank you, thank you again for a most sensational
experience. I simply do not know how to begin to give
an account of it all – it was just such fun. It started to
be fun the minute Jenny Hicks Beach rang me when
in London to suggest we share a minicab to Heathrow,
so that was how we met; none of the others seemed to
know each other already, though most of Amelia's* [the
travel lady arranging the trip on behalf of the cruise
line] *twelve were friends of yours and were there at
your most fantastic invitation. We joined the ship at
'Dar' and the heavenly, heavenly hot weather began.
My cabin was amazing! I was expecting one with
portholes, as shown in the brochure, but no, it was the
best huge double cabin called 'St Ewe', just behind the
Reception desk but on the port side (of course, Port
Out Starboard Home), king-size bed, and big beautiful windows, and such a bathroom with triangular
bath with every luxury included and no single room
supplement.*

That evening we had the Purser's cocktail party, and Amelia introduced us to each other, and where the scene was set for flowing Champagne or indeed anything you could possibly think of to ask for. It did not seem to matter if there was a party or not, we all met every evening for drinks before dinner in the main lounge. There I learned what 'duty free' means in this remarkable ship: as a lone female, but well trained by my Royal Navy background to always travel with a bottle of gin for emergencies; one can then order tonic water, fresh iced limejuice or whatever from the bar, and lace it discreetly from one's own source. Imagine my surprise when I joined our party before dinner to find them all drinking dry Martinis which were 'on the house'; we then all staggered down to dinner where unlimited wine washed everything down.

The visit to Wasini Island the first day is worthy of note; there we had enormous land crab served with a hammer (to attack the shell) in an open air restaurant, shaded by a thatched roof where thousands of bats sheltered from the sun by hanging upside down from the rafters; the dhow trip to reach the snorkelling area across the pale green, delectably warm sea was a delight. When we got there, Jenny and I were towed, holding on to a rubber ring, held by a Swahili who took us to all the best coral areas to see the exquisite shoals of multi-coloured fish – I managed to fry my back which is only now recovering! My own fault for not wearing a shirt. Future snorkelling was less successful and several times I had to be rescued when found swimming great guns in the direction of Ceylon. Amelia's party managed to be endlessly entertaining. Johnny Shaw was most likely to be late or left behind because he had suddenly decided to climb a light house or almost anything else worth climbing. He went ashore on one island in his dressing gown. His wife had a hard time retrieving him and often thought he was beside her, waiting for the boat, only to discover he had vanished again. Another most entertaining character, always having to be dragged out of shops to catch the last boat back to the ship was Jane Wansborough, who shopped till she dropped, buying amazing local output and more and bigger baskets to put them in; she also had a delightful solo cabaret act which she would be unable to resist performing whenever Martin the musical genius on board burst into suitable music. She came as a friend of Simon Williams Thomas, another lunatic character to whom I became much attached, and who also had splendid entertainment value. There was a wealth of talent on board and Johnny wrote an exquisite wild west script (lasted 8 minutes) in which Simon excelled and David Selby was the star; David is the funniest and nicest person, and kept producing yet one more exotic cocktail, which has got me into very bad habits; Sue was also the greatest fun, her mother it seems lives near me in London and we are to meet. The parties after dinner on the mizzen, accompanied by Martin and his keyboard, were very much better than watching telly; their endlessly inventive and idiotic behaviour as the night progressed often ended with someone, usually Jane, jumping into the swimming pool with all her clothes on; one night she forgot her cabin key so, unable to get into her cabin, she curled up in the passageway and went to sleep, being rescued next morning by 'snakehips', one of the ship's officers, named for his amazing dancing technique.

Another night Jenny damaged her knee and had to be conveyed to her cabin in a wheelchair by the doctor, who was also a rather amusing character. Being much the oldest of the group, I used to stay up to enjoy their antics until it seemed time to go to bed, and so I missed some of the better moments, but I firmly refused to take part in the dancing except for 'Strip the Willow', which we took at high speed and I managed to stay vertical. Johnny told me I was nick-named Miss Marple by the others, but though I was flattered, I explained that I needed a dead body to do justice to my role.

A post picnic walk.

Going ashore was exciting with the huge swell of the Indian Ocean and the Captain was always at hand to see us safely on and off boats – usually zodiacs rubber dinghies. There was a moment when we crashed into the ship, the fender proving inadequate. He showed huge professionalism deciding whether the weather was just possible or impossible, I should not have liked to make his decision with some of the rest of the passengers in mind, who were neither sylph-like nor nim-

ble. *Incidentally, we none of us dared to speak to any of the real cruisers who had paid the full £9,000 in case we gave our secret away.*

The BBQs and picnics on the unbelievably beautiful palm tree islands fringed with translucent sea were all of a very high order: beautifully laid-out tables, shaded by the sea grape trees, with delicious food and drinks brought from the ship, and, thoughtfully, towels for the swimmers. One very memorable picnic when most of us were still in the water, the head steward decided to bring our glasses of iced Champagne to us in the sea, wading up to his armpits with the tray aloft, which really celebrated the height of decadence. I forget that you have done these cruises four times, dear Vanessa, but you may like to be reminded of it all by a first-time partaker.

The height of decadence – pre-picnic champagne.

Have I mentioned Sara Stewart and Ian Agnew? They make a most distinguished-looking couple and also good fun in a slightly more restrained way. Ian has such a wonderful deep voice, almost a growl, very valuable in the cabarets; he led a near mutiny when we were sailing along after two days at sea past a very desirable island where we wished to go ashore and swim – we all signed his petition, but the Captain was adamant, no going ashore with the strong wind and tides prevailing. Sara is just so beautiful and wore the most heavenly clothes, it was a constant pleasure to look at her. Ian took part in some of the review acts when a very large bang or explosion was required some distance from the scene of action – at which he excelled.

I even found myself playing bridge just after breakfast one day; Johnny Shaw would pounce on the nearest player to hand and go on until a natural interruption such as lunch, or a lecture or quiz. No very serious bridge player took part.

Amelia was amazing, quietly organising anything that needed it and inventing most imaginative ways of using our time to best advantage – such as the long wait on our last day at Nairobi, where she found we could fit in a safari, conveniently placed just outside the town; two minibuses picked us up at the airport and between 3 pm and 7 pm we drove miles through this real, wild African country inhabited by all the animals one expects to see in this continent, followed by a farewell dinner at the restaurant where we could eat all the creatures we had just seen. She was always ahead of me in thinking up less athletic ways for me to enjoy everything. Hugo, her son, is a remarkable young man, talented artist and a great asset to the whole party, another new friend.

I could go on forever but I guess you get the picture. I send this to you post haste, while it is fresh in *my mind and to give you a first-hand account of what we all needed you both to be part of. I forget what day you will be back from Burma but it must be any minute. Thank you, thank you a million times again and much love –*

Christian

Strokes of luck like this do not come often, but one can keep a good look out for them.

I might never have heard of *La Compagnie du Ponant* if Amelia Dalton (whose firm, Travel by Design, creates bespoke holidays) had not steered me in their direction. They have three ships, all built in and managed from France, which take you to the most exotic parts of the world, but only one of them – the smallest – has sails. None of them are large and the only one I can tell you about first-hand is *Le Ponant*. She accommodates 64 passengers with 30 or so crew. The three vast masts have sail area of 16,000 square feet, and she proceeds at the rate of (about) 15 knots, the canvas contributing an extra three.

Travelling has always been a passion with me and my intention is always to enjoy every minute of it from the first second after I close my front door behind me. Two weeks in boiling weather in January sets me up for the rest of our filthy English climate. There are good and bad things about most parts of the world, but when I saw *Le Ponant* was going to sail gently round the Seychelles and Amirante Islands, offering first-class snorkelling – another of my passions – every day in the blissful tranquil waters of the aqua-marine Indian Ocean, I knew I had to go. When I noticed that the cruise was for only one week, I rang up and said: 'I am not going all that way for a week, I will do the whole cruise twice.'

I have discovered that even 'checking in' at airports can be a pleasure; you might be a 'frequent flier' and have access to the very desirable Executive Lounge, or it is possible by luck or by lashing out extra cash to be upgraded to Club Class; I did once, rather bravely, try to bribe the superior young man at the desk, but he waved my £50-note aside with a smile and upgraded me anyway. There is another way, but only for those who are not too proud to admit to the failings of *Anno Domini* – you can ask for 'Assistance', which costs nothing. This will give you the double fun of sailing about the airport in a white, leather-upholstered motorised buggy, overtaking all other passengers as it sweeps you to the front of the queue; your passport is taken from you and used as a talisman at all gates of security, resulting in your effortless arrival at the Executive Lounge, where you can treat yourself to your first large free celebratory drink. However, I have to say that on this particular cruise I made a bad mistake by flying via Paris, where 'Assistance' is not free and where I was very nearly left behind while being assured that departure was not imminent, when it actually was. I was the last to board and as I took my seat, the door immediately clanged shut behind me and we took off!

The moment of arrival at Seychelles Airport when you step out into the no-nonsense heat is to be anticipated with impatience. My next excitement was a short bus ride for the passengers through the island of Mahé, named by the French in honour of the 18th-century Governor of Mauritius. It is the largest island of the Seychelles archipelago (4 by 16 miles), granitic and mountainous, the highest peak there being Morne Seychellois at 2,969 feet, and 90 percent of the population live there. It exports copra, cinnamon bark, leaf oil, and vanilla, and it also grows tea. Victoria is the Republic's capital and only port. The town square boasts a large clock, optimistically called Big Ben, which we drove past before arriving at the quay; here, alongside the jetty, and much bigger than I expected, lay the elegant, streamlined ship *Le Ponant* waiting for me. There were other passengers of course, but all French, and I had yet to meet them.

Leaving Mahe harbour.

Soon there was the thrill of my cabin; it had a porthole, in front of which was a beautiful single scarlet anthurium lily with one elegant leaf in a stem-like vase. Although most of the space was occupied by a large, comfortable-looking bed – I quickly checked the pillows, and yes, they were real down – there was a small dressing table with very big mirror and frig with mini-bar. The shower room was tiny but brilliantly contained the essentials of life. I am completely hopeless at all plumbing controls; here they looked simple enough even for me. Another plus was my favourite Roget and Gallet soap and shower-gels – and a little sewing kit in case of disaster.

A blast from the very powerful foghorn brought me to my senses and I hurried up the gangway to observe our departure from the deck. Most of the passengers were already on the sundeck, from where operations were conducted by the captain. The ship glided smoothly from the dockside and, making a huge U-turn, headed out to sea. At the press of several automated buttons on the computerised bridge control – no powder monkeys required here – all five of the sails reeved obediently up the masts and filled to perfection as we ran before the wind. I intended to spend a great deal of time on this sundeck, which was shaded by a big awning and where fruit juice and coffee were available – there were inviting *'chaises longues'* stacked up for future use; reading in the shade on deck was what I came for, and among the several books I looked forward most to reading was *Agent Zigzag*, by Ben Macintyre. It was a thriller spy story and written in such an exciting way that the minute I had finished it, I had to start reading it all over again – this does not happen to me very often. Lunch was served that first day on the deck above, very good smoked dorade served hot with chard, and fruit for pudding, wine included of course – in reality you were in France now!

Le Ponant awaits our return.

Soon after sailing we had the lifeboat drill – careful instructions for putting on life jackets – so now we all knew what to do and where to go if we heard the dreaded call of 'Abandon Ship'.

All this time I had been observing my companions; French of course, and mostly in pairs, in their forties and fifties at a guess, taking a break from their very successful business enterprises. Their clothes were the latest fashion and the best, and I would enjoy that over the course of the trip. Two couples stood nearest me – one man had a very bushy beard with a small and square wife; another nice-looking woman with a completely bald husband; and nearby a lady on her own – all quite promising. I have various techniques when travelling alone, one of which is to arrive last for dinner, and here I found the head waiter, Grégoire, also has his strategy: seeing that I was sometimes debating which table to join, he would come over and take my arm, and together we would choose a likely place for me to dine – thus, importantly, not only had I made friends with Grégoire but also with several of the passengers.

Captain Reggie ran a very tight ship, and his team all appeared to like each other and get on. I noted the way the crew were meticulous about their duties; the boat boys tidied everything up, hosed down the deck and rearranged all the chairs; they all seemed to be friends and were matey with us passengers as well. Another great plus about this ship was the way one could swim from the stern, whenever the captain found a suitable place. In a matter of minutes, the steps and security lines would be put in place and we would just step into the ocean.

That first night there was a party, so we all dolled ourselves up, filled our glasses and the music played; then the captain did his party trick, which was slicing off the top of the champagne bottle with his sword – very impressive. He then danced with everyone, including his staff – no wonder the ship ran so smoothly. That night I found myself at the captain's table for dinner; we had first-class lobster bisque – the richest kind of soup – *pâté de foie gras*, followed by two or three kinds of fish and meat, all washed down with several choices of wine. I observed that the captain only drank water – he said his wife made up for him!

I had taken the precaution of presenting copies of my two gardening books to the ship's library – *From the Ends of the Earth: Passionate plant collectors remembered in a Cornish garden* and *This Infant Adventure: Offspring of the Royal Gardens at Kew* – and as luck would have it, the captain turned out to be a passionate gardener himself, so that broke the ice; his English was very good, and while my French was coming back (having spent a year in France just before the war, I had been bilingual), he politely slowed down the other guests' conversation so I could keep up. A few days later, as we glided over the bluest of seas, miles from anywhere in the Indian Ocean, you could observe Reggie and myself sitting on deck over a drink, while on his laptop he showed me pictures of his garden in Normandy.

We voyaged from island to island, sometimes with all sails, sometimes not – the ship had a most enjoyable roll. We anchored off while the zodiac rubber dinghies plied to and fro, taking people to the beach on exploring trips with our onboard Seychelloise naturalist, Gemma, and for barbecues, swimming, snorkelling and picnics, all very relaxed. I had visited the islands before in *Hebridean Spirit*, so I knew that Aride was one island I had to see again. A philanthropic Mr Cadbury had bought the island some time ago to conserve it for the birds, and having rid it entirely of rats and cats, the birds nested quite safely on the ground or even under the roots of trees – they showed no fear of us as we prowled round their habitat.

There was also a particular primadonna of a plant I had planned to visit, *Wright's gardenia*, which is indigenous to and only grows on this island. It is temperamental, like all primadonnas, and will only flower exactly ten days after rain. I consulted with Gemma who promised to telephone ahead and find out if the omens were propitious. If I had realised that it lived three-quarters of the way up a mountain, I would have thought twice about the expedition, but having heard that it was indeed just coming into bloom, I felt obliged to take part in the adventure. It was a very hairy climb over big boulders and steep slippery tracks but there it was, one elegant little white flower with red stripes, waiting to have its photograph taken. Somehow I managed the even worse descent, but felt, as Monsieur Michelin would say, '*ça vaut le détour*'.

The Indian Ocean always has quite a strong swell, so every day Lucie, the expert diving and snorkelling crew member who became another valued friend, would lead us to the best area for this activity, having reconnoitred it earlier that morning; she would take us through some quite bumpy seas to wonderful deep rocky caverns where one could observe the antics of exotic fish – shining, brilliant black and white, or green and white stripes with scarlet fins – or to an underwater paradise where you might find yourself in the very middle of a shoal of thousands of very pale blue creatures, who seemed quite unconcerned by any non-fishy presence. There were turtles and parrot fish and even baby sharks; there were also tricky moments getting in and out of the boat. It was a blissful way to spend a chunk of gloomy January.

The tortoise seemed to hardly notice me sitting on it.

Curieuse was another interesting island whose speciality was giant tortoises; they are not very communicative so all you can do is offer them some little titbit which they may or may not deign to accept. Some of our party did try to ride on them but I doubt if the tortoises even noticed. The swimming was good from the beach and Grégoire supplied us with drinks, which were served from an anchored kayak.

There was one other island of note we had to see, Praslin, where the enormous and unique sea coconut, or *coco de mer*, is conserved, and a party of us went by zodiac to inspect its special habitat. It is the sole member of the genus *Lodoicea* and is endemic to the island; it grows to 30 metres with huge fan-shaped leaves ten metres long by five metres wide; the flowers are the largest of any palm and it produces the biggest fruit in the plant kingdom (curiously shaped like the human bottom), of which the largest so far recorded weighed 42 kilograms. This vast seedpod is known as the Love Nut – among other names – and many replicas of it are made and sold as souvenirs.

After a final party the first week's cruise was over, and the other passengers disembarked while I spent the day exploring Mahé, hiring a car for the day with a driver called Sampsi. I did a little shopping, had lunch, and then he drove me over mountainous roads, stopping now and again to study local plants, cinnamon and ylang-ylang (the scent plant); there were tea plantations, a long deep mangrove swamp, umbrella trees (*Albizia*), a huge red clay quarry, and wonderful views of the sea and the islands. Sampsi thought I ought to see a very old cemetery with a memorial to a 14-year-old giant and some old graves in a very pretty setting; after this it was time to return to the ship and meet the new passengers for the other half of the cruise.

The second week was just a repeat of the first, but my diary is ecstatic about the colour of the blissfully warm sea, while aiming in sometimes quite heavy swell for the dramatic rocks where the secretive but exotic fish were to be found. I much appreciated the way the captain and crew behaved like old friends, always looking after me, making sure I didn't miss any of the best snorkelling. In between times I indulged in my other favourite occupation – reading on deck in the shade of the sails; I would always wait for the sunset, which filled the whole horizon with its vibrant colour, changing very quickly from glowing red, paling to pink, and finally waiting for the green flash which only occasionally happened.

Farewell drinks and dinner being over, I packed and prepared for a very early start for home next day. There was only one flight from Mahé to Paris, and the first inkling of disaster told us there was also only one aircraft and the flight would be delayed half an hour owing to technical trouble. Our cruise director left us in the hands of the airport manager and rushed off to meet and greet the new passengers arriving for the next cruise.

Alas for us, we watched all the signs of a deteriorating situation; the worst, which caused considerable alarm, was when they towed the blighted aircraft up and down the only runway in front of us, trying to make it start – we felt like rushing out to help by giving it a push! Our confidence plunged further when it disappeared into its hangar; the management gave up the monotonous, periodic announcements which told us of yet another further delay and told us of its cancellation; to our dismay all the luggage was taken off and no flight promised until at least the next day.

We were then embarked in a bus and driven miles and miles – at least an hour – to a hotel called the Plantation Hotel and Casino. Here the worst queue was for the telephone – we were only allowed one call each – for just three minutes; we all battered away at the information desk to try and find out our fate or get a flight – to anywhere. No one would tell us anything except that the airport had now closed down. It took three days of this uncertainty before a serviceable aircraft was found; heaven alone knew whether it was the same old crate or a new one – we would have flown in anything with wings – and we were told to expect take-off at midnight. No one had bothered to update our tickets, so on arrival at Charles de Gaulle I discovered that, although my suitcase was booked on my scheduled flight to London, I was not! It took all my 50-year-old French to bully a bolshy lot of frogs into resolving this situation, and I was thankful to arrive at Heathrow triumphant.

THE
KERALA COAST OF
INDIA

Choosing from *Le Ponant*'s cruises the following year, I could only find one which suited me and that was over Christmas and New Year. The ship was sailing on 21st December from Bombay (now Mumbai) and exploring the Kerala coast, which always sounds romantic and interesting. Before I went, and so as not to abandon all Christmas festivities, I invited all my children and grandchildren, and the three little greats – 17 in all – to lunch at the Sloane Club in Chelsea, from where it was easy to be on my way and dropped off at Heathrow.

I had never been to Bombay but had heard from my grandmother how she, at the age of 18 and suitably chaperoned, in 1888, had sailed there from England – literally under sail in those days – to be married to her young Doctor who worked for the British Government. It was quite a saga: when, after their marriage, they settled down in his remote place of work, there was an epidemic of cholera; in spite of taking all precautions and segregating himself, he caught it and died of it. Thus leaving his young widow, pregnant with my mother, to produce her baby with only her ayah to help, and to face the daunting journey back to Bombay and from there the long voyage home. I planned to include the Cathedral where she was married in my tour of the city.

Banyan Tours met me and we had a whole day for seeing the sights before joining the ship at teatime. After the Cathedral we visited Victoria Station, which resembled Saint Pancras and which is used by seven million people daily, travelling to and from work. There was a good deal of squalor in the city, with families sleeping in the streets and makeshift camping arrangements throughout; one huge area is dedicated to *dhobi*, or washing, where you can see acres of white garments blowing in the wind. My camera chose that minute to jamb, which was a pity.

Le Ponant looked very small in the huge docks, but it was a pleasure to go on board once more. Sadly there was no one from the previous cruise among the crew so I had to start breaking the ice all over again. This happened very quickly as Christmas was upon us and the festivities began almost at once. We all warmed to the captain when a fishing line snarled the propeller – quite undaunted he put on his bathers and dived over the stern with his assistant, and unsnarled it in no time.

I made great friends with a French passenger called Regina; we always seemed to be lying on deck reading and she told me that her cruise had started at Marseilles and she had booked as far as Bombay, but as she was enjoying herself so much, she decided to stay on indefinitely. I was impressed – there were definitely worse ways to spend your life than moving into a permanent French restaurant which sailed around the world.

On Christmas Eve, preparations for the festive season soon began: champagne on the sundeck at 8 pm and the new captain did the same party trick of slicing off the cork with his sword! The second officer dressed as Father Christmas, climbed to the crow's nest and descended with his sack of goodies, then, escorted by all the crew, presented us with our chosen gifts. I was invited to dine at the captain's table and managed to get through a vast number of delicious courses, all of which took most of the evening. The African chef came round afterwards to be congratulated and embraced by everyone.

Christmas Day itself was celebrated at sea with carols and seasonal music played through the loudspeaker system, punctuated by further considerable eating and drinking; later, when everybody was dressed up for the evening, we had another superb dinner. The party continued on the lower deck and as suitable music played, the young – and even the not so young – began to divert us with wild and exotic dancing; when they tired of this, they plunged into the sea (the steps and life lines having being prepared in anticipation); one of the passengers even dared to push the captain in – still in his party clothes – who took this *'lèse majesté'* in good part.

Christmas day – swimming off the stern of the boat.

Early on Boxing Day we arrived at the port of Trivandrum; the captain had told us we must be up early in time to see the sensational fishing fleet return at sunrise. The narrow entrance to the port required *Le Ponant* to do a neat dogleg turn into the only berth available. The huge crowd of colourful vessels streamed past us on their return from their night's fishing; that evening we waited

The Trivandrum fleet on their return from a night's fishing.

for them to set out again about five o'clock.

Trivandrum is a very special place and a bus had been arranged to pick us all up on arrival to view the sights. Among them was the Palace Museum, where we had to take off our shoes to walk round an enormous building filled with life-size statues of gods (green gods good, red and blue ones bad); the roof was most amazing with life-size teak and rosewood carvings of horses' heads decorating the edges with some elephant trunks and lions' paws for variation – there were acres and acres of it. After this marathon, I went on strike and refused to visit the next sight, the Napier Museum; instead, I and another passenger sat in a shady garden where we could recover and admire the plants. A whole school of children came by and seemed to view us as zoo exhibits, taking endless photos of us in different poses.

Next day I took the morning off sightseeing and parked myself on deck as usual in the delicious boiling shade. I felt very much at home while the cheerful officers and crew, who all seemed to be on most friendly terms, rushed about their duties, cleaning the decks, scrubbing everywhere and everything, as well as polishing the bright work – I found it very soothing. The ship was always meticulously clean.

The sightseers returned punctually at 12.30 for lunch, which was served on deck. Meals are taken very seriously by the French; there were some memorable stomachs on this cruise and when you observed the 'frogs' with their feet – as it were – in the trough, it was quite impressive. (I often refer to the French as 'frogs', to which they retaliate by calling us '*rosbifs*'.) Even at lunch time and in this considerable heat, they managed to down at least three courses from the buffet, often with second helpings – mounds of smoked fish, fat prawns, varieties of meat, asparagus, salads, followed by particularly choice cheese and finishing with highly decorated puddings – all washed down with rosé wine served with ice cubes.

Arriving at Kochi, the next port of call, I went ashore to explore. Here the first week of the cruise ended and new passengers embarked late in the day. I had a car booked and arranged for a guide, Agita, to accompany me. We decided to drive through Fort Kochi, visiting a small Palais Dutch on the way. This Mattancherry Palace was actually built by the Portuguese and gifted as a present to the Raja of Cochin about 1555. The Dutch carried out renovations in 1663 and it then became popularly known as the Palais Dutch. The glory of the place rests in the large number of murals executed in the best traditions of the Hindu temple art, which are religious, decorative and stylised, painted in rich warm colours in tempera technique. They are notable as some of the best mythological murals in India. The palace is a masterpiece, showcasing the blend between colonial and Kerala architecture. Among interesting exhibits are an ivory palanquin, a howdah, royal umbrellas, and ceremonial dress used by royalty.

I photographed some huge 400-year-old rain trees (*Samanea saman*), which were originally brought from Brazil by the Portuguese and planted as avenues all those years ago.

The fishing beaches were most intriguing, where the equipment was operated by about seven men hauling on ropes which had huge boulders to weight them down, attached to fishing nets which descend as the men haul up the ropes; they do this frequently when the tide is right and bring up small quantities of fish (or none) each time. The Arabian Sea waters are tidal and they alternate with the fresh waters rushing down from about 40 rivers from the mountains of Kerala; some of the fish can't live in fresh water, so retreat with the tide; others adapt and can live in either.

On the approach to Kochi there is an island formed entirely of the silt dredged when the harbour was prepared to shelter ships coming from the Suez Canal. It was finished about 1930 and no one lives there, but huge import-export businesses and offices are based on it.

Moving inland we found a small fortress, supposed to have been the Maharajah's Coronation Palace, and in the garden were two splendid male elephants with fine tusks, who looked, as only elephants can, as if they were in charge. I have always had a great admiration for these wonderful creatures since I read a book called *Elephant Bill* by J.H. Williams. Colonel Williams, having devoted more than 20 years to Indian elephants, became the most famous of elephant officers during World War II in Burma. He describes their remarkable characters and how there is always a leading animal in a group – very often a female. This was demonstrated on such an occasion when our valuable team of working elephants was in danger of being captured by the Japanese. The southern route was compromised, so the only way out of Burma into India meant a perilous journey through the foothills of the Himalayas. Colonel Williams reconnoitred the only possible path with his head elephant man, Po Toke, who announced that:

> '*Bandoola* [a male in this instance] *will lead and if he won't face it none of the others will ... and if he should refuse halfway up, he can back all the way down – he has eyes in his backside.*'

The path they had to take was along a very narrow ledge, with sheer cliff above and below, until the top was reached; they had actually cut a series of steps in the sandstone, each just big enough to take an elephant's foot. During the action, Bill recounts:

> *'Bandoola's head and tusks suddenly came round the corner below me – he looked almost as though he was standing on his hind legs; the oozie [mahout] was sitting on his head, looking down and seemed to be directing the elephant where to place his feet, then he passed the worst place – we had got Bandoola up at least halfway.'*

Po Toke was right – they all followed. Bill adds:

> *'I waited and ticked off forty-five adult elephants and eight calves at heel go by. The back legs of some of the animals had been strained to such a point that they would not stop quivering.'*

It seems very likely, though I cannot be sure, that feelings of loyalty were involved, and Bandoola, having bravely taken the first step, ensured that our string of elephants escaped.

Leaving the elephants to their own devices, Agita and I drove through a little narrow street of shops; the grand ones usually had Western loos, so were necessary ports of call. In the smart carpet shop I had great difficulty in resisting the very persuasive salesman from selling me several handsome rugs. After a rather peculiar lunch – I had an Indian sandwich and Agita a local rice dish – she wanted to show me more of the countryside, so we explored rice fields in the backwaters of mangrove swamps, where there were egrets, cormorants, terns and kites to be seen.

Agita explained how Kerala is a very peaceful place in spite of its many religions; Jainites, for instance, can't kill anything, so no meat, fish or eggs, not even root vegetables for them, as pulling up their roots is tantamount to murder. The residents consist of about 40 percent Christians, 30 percent Muslims, and about the same of Hindus – only 11 Jews left. They all get on extremely well and often have arranged marriages; the girls have to be virgins, marry within their own religions, get big dowries and have two children each. It is a very family-orientated place, with good school facilities; Agita told me that most people pay for their children's schooling; she was doing her job of guiding to save up for her own children (this encouraged me to add to her tip). The caste system is out of date and the socialist-communist attitude is very popular. There were no beggars lying about the streets.

The next day I joined the group with the new passengers and visited Kochi again. The main object of this tour was to explore the town's backwaters, which are amazing. It was an hour and a half bus ride, climbing through wooded hillside; the wide, tidal river ran between acres of rice fields and the local population lived in small houses near the river banks, and on the edges one could observe ladies bashing their washing in true Indian style. The huge waterways were very busy with boats of all sorts, but particularly many of the type on which we were about to embark for our day trip. These vessels were most attractive and cool with bamboo roofs and arched windows; the restaurant where we were to have lunch was arranged like an old-fashioned train, so we sat in rows. There were two bedrooms as well, with nice clean bathrooms; they served a buffet curry lunch, which went down well with beer.

Overnight we sailed to the Maldive Islands – plenty of time for me and Regina, the perpetual cruiser, to lie on deck as usual, either reading our books or discussing every subject under the sun as sometimes one finds it possible to do with a complete stranger.

The Republic of the Maldives is an island nation in the Indian Ocean about 470 miles south-west of Sri Lanka and 370 miles south-west of India. The Portuguese and the Dutch ruled there briefly, but it became a British Protectorate from 1887 until 1965. It is the smallest Asian country in population and land area, and is the planet's lowest country. Forecasts predicting inundation due to rising sea levels are of great concern to its people.

My favourite occupation on deck.

Here were supposed to be the best beaches in the world, and it is a favourite place for weddings and honeymoons. The swimming was wonderful and we had excellent barbecues. If there was good snorkelling, we did not find it after several disappointing expeditions. From here we left the ship and flew home to our various destinations.

The captain navigates us safely through the narrow channel guided by info from his masthead look-out.

It was not long after this that these Indian Ocean waters became prey to Somali pirates and *Le Ponant* was one of their first victims as she was sailing from the Seychelles to Yemen to pick up passengers. In fact, it was this very same year, 2008, that it happened; Somali pirates in the Gulf of Aden spotted her, the luxury 32-cabin, three-masted sailing yacht, with only a crew of 30 on board; the Somalis thought they had hit the jackpot, and three of them headed for her in a speedboat firing automatic weapons, to which the crew responded with fire hoses – all they had. A second speedboat with six more pirates soon joined in, and together they swarmed all over the ship, eventually taking control. The female members of the crew were locked in a hold where they were forced to stay for two days, while the yacht was sailed by the pirates for Garaad (a village in Somalia's region of Puntland). By this time there were French Navy vessels following at a discreet distance.

The pirates feared attacks by rival clans when they arrived, so more guns were brought on board and about 30 people, both pirates and villagers, took turns at guard duty. The pirates settled in for the next few days and, according to one member of the crew, even brought four live goats on board, slaughtered them and had a barbecue; the hostages were followed everywhere, including to the bathroom. Piracy is a very lucrative business off this coast, so the kidnappers treated their captives well in anticipation of a good ransom. Eventually US $2 million were paid by the ship's owner and the crew was then released and taken on board a French navy ship. Soon after this, French commandos carried out a helicopter raid, intercepted the 4x4 vehicle and captured the armed pirates as they fled by car into the Somali desert. Unfortunately they were part of a bigger gang, so only $200,000 was recovered, the other pirates having got away with most of the ransom. Six of the Somalis were eventually put on trial in Paris – one of them admitted piracy, two said they were on board, but only to sell goats and cigarettes, and the others denied ever being on board. If convicted they face life in prison.

Not surprisingly this area in the Gulf of Aden is given a somewhat wider berth by cruise ships these days.

I must admit that it was the description of *Sea Cloud* rather than where she was going that attracted me the following year: about three times the size of *Le Ponant* (but still only taking 60 or so passengers), she is a square rigger of immense grandeur. She was built as a barque in 1931 in Kiel, Germany and launched as *Hussar II*, the largest private yacht in the world for the financier E.F. Hutton and his cereal (some sort of cornflakes, I believe) heiress wife, Marjorie Merriweather Post. The ship was designed (with money no object) to dazzle all who saw her, and featured unheard-of technologies, such as watertight compartmentalisation, found up to then only in submarines; yet towering above the teak decks and mahogany cabin structures was the nearly 200-feet-high rig of a late 19th-century four-masted barque, one of the largest sailing ships that ever plied the trade wind routes.

Sea Cloud had had a chequered career before becoming a luxurious five-star cruise ship; the Huttons lived in her for many years, but in 1935, the US Ambassador to the Soviet Union, Joseph E.

Davies, obtained her by marrying Hutton's now ex-wife (Marjorie Merriweather Post), and renamed the ship '*Sea Cloud*'. When the war came, she was made use of in various ways; she was chartered as a weather ship for $1 per year by the US Coast Guard and US Navy, and served as the first integrated warship in the US Armed Forces since the American Civil War. She then returned to private ownership as a yacht for various people, including as the Presidential Yacht of the Dominican Republic. Now, with an extra deck added, she sailed as part of a fleet of sail cruise ships, operated by Sea Cloud Cruises of Hamburg, Germany, often under contract to the National Geographic Society.

The Sea Cloud – a luxurious five-star cruise ship with a glamorous history.

The most expensive cabins with vast double beds, marble bathrooms and antique furniture, each uniquely designed, were to be found right down below deck in what I call the bilges. But Marjorie chose this area where the Huttons were to live, knowing that it would have minimum roll. At the end of each cruise, all the passengers were invited to view the ten opulent apartments while sipping a glass or two of champagne. I much preferred my (cheaper) cabin on the new upper deck, where I could sit over my breakfast in bed and gaze at the sea through a big square window, occasionally catching sight of flying fish or dolphins frolicking.

British Airways took me direct to Antigua and the ship sailed as soon as the passengers were all on board; when the pilot had finished assisting our departure, the cruise director Angelica assembled us on the Lido deck to explain the sail-setting procedure, describing how they would 'brace the yards' depending on the course and direction of the wind. The furling and unfurling of the sails is done in the rigging, the setting as well as the dousing (taking in the sails) is handled from the deck. Evocative words like 'set the lower and upper topsails', 'set topgallants and royals', 'gibes' and 'staysails' and 'spanker' painted the atmosphere. She had a spellbound audience. Angelica was German, as were many of the crew, so everything had to be translated. The captain was American, his first officer Russian, other officers Polish, Montenegrin, Austrian and German. The bosun and his mostly Filipino sailors were always busy, scampering up and down the yards, adjusting the sails, polishing the bright work, painting and maintaining the yards, stays and rigging. Passengers were always welcome on the bridge unless the ship was entering or leaving port. I gave a copy of my recently written book – *I Only Joined for the Hat: Redoubtable Wrens at War* – to the ship's library, and was thrilled when the captain said he was enjoying reading it. I often chatted to him when watching manoeuvres from the bridge, asking him such questions as how far *Sea Cloud* heeled over in a storm; he said usually only 10 or 12 degrees, but she could keel over to 80 degrees without capsizing. I was relieved to hear it. Our usual speed under sail was about 10 or 11 knots, which the engines could boost to 14 if required.

I am sorry to say I have always been a fair-weather sailor and so the West Indies was my idea of heaven; the wind rarely changed direction, so that when you had chosen your sunny or shady site – I found a lovely place called the monkey deck, just above the bridge – you could settle down with your book and maybe your drink. Unlike dinghies – my usual form of sailing – the *Sea Cloud* never seemed to undertake manoeuvres such as going-about or gibing; when I mentioned gibing to the bosun he went a little pale – I gathered this was not something *Sea Cloud* did and he explained what occurred if this tactic became necessary, but he lost me very quickly.

When my husband John left the Royal Navy and retired to Cornwall to become Harbourmaster of Par – a very small but busy port – we had to decide what was the cheapest form of entertainment for ourselves and our three children, who were all at boarding school; buying a second-hand Enterprise dinghy seemed to be the answer. John, like many naval officers, had never done much of this sort of sailing, except from his ship when sailors would rig the boat and all he would have to do was pull a small piece of string and sail off to wherever – if he didn't return, search parties would be sent out to find him. No such luxuries were available now, and we were on our own. Sailing is rather like the card game Bridge – it's a sport where husband and wife are best separated. I soon became a passionate gardener instead. John kept the boat for free in his Port of Par and did a lot of sailing with the children and his Yacht Club friends.

The weather was always good during my two magical weeks in the Caribbean; the ship rolled delightfully at night, though there were occasionally sort of scraping noises, as if we might be going aground. I wondered whether I should remember how to put on my life jacket – we had had a very lifelike rehearsal for 'Abandon Ship', not to mention 'Man Overboard'. During the latter I asked a crew member if they had managed to fish out the victim and he told me they had had to stop trying as it was lunch time! Just as well it was an exercise.

Our itinerary was planned to avoid the big, well-frequented harbours where the monster floating hotels could tie up to the jetties and spill their touristy contents ashore in their thousands. Instead, *Sea Cloud* concentrated on smaller, more exclusive and expensive resorts (much frequented by pirates in days of yore), which are standard in the British Virgin Islands, and so she entered the narrow gulf into Virgin Gorda Sound between two spectacular reefs and anchored at one of the best known, Bitter End Yacht Club, accessible only from the sea. Sailing here is the foremost activity and yachtsmen find the perfect combination of trade winds in waters protected from the long Atlantic swell. This island is best known for the Baths, about a mile down Millionaire's Road from Spanish Town, which is the small capital. A special tender took us to Little Gun Creek Marina, where we were met by safari trucks (charming little buses with open sides) for our ride across the island. The Baths are an astonishing sight; it is as if a giant hand had flung Herculean boulders, like granite marbles, across the white sand of a cove; the sea rushes in to form a labyrinth of crystal-clear channels and pools. In some trepidation I approached the pale, aquamarine, enticing sea, only to be violently washed up by enormous waves like so much flotsam.

Swimming, barbecues, excursions to see old forts, botanic gardens, abandoned sugar mills and other sights of interest were all part of our delectable cruise round these historic islands, some of which had changed hands during the Napoleonic Wars as many as 22 times. Isles des Saintes, which remains French, has chic boutiques and restaurants. There is another ravishing beach about a 20-minute hot walk across the island, which is very popular with goats, who of course are known to eat anything. If you wish to risk it and swim you must hang your towel and clothes high up on a grape tree or post a goat-watch.

Most of the passengers on this voyage were American, always friendly and willing to chat; there was quite a large clique of Germans who always sat together at meals and were difficult to penetrate. There was only one English couple and strangely they had a house not far from mine in Cornwall. We made instant friends and have remained in frequent contact.

I must have sent about 19 postcards, graphically describing our wonderful prowess, and was rather flattered to find on my return a reply from a grandson saying:

'*You must be the most mobile and adventurous Great Granny in the world!*'

I would do it all again.

THE CLOUD FOREST
OF COSTA RICA

Costa Rica is a Mecca for all nature lovers, having a huge variety of known and unknown mammals, reptiles, birds, bats, butterflies, insects and plants – *par excellence*. It lies ten degrees north of the equator, and is part of the thin land link between North and South America that also forms the narrow isthmus between the Pacific and Atlantic oceans. Four mountain ranges divide the east from the west and on the Pacific side of the southernmost range of Talamanca lies the magical Monteverde Cloud Forest Reserve. Trade winds from the Atlantic force moist air up the mountains, cooling as it rises, which condenses to create clouds. Here is the ideal home for an abundance of plants, where the tree trunks and branches are covered in dense blankets of mosses and lichens, twisting vines, fallen trees and giant tree ferns.

Lindblad/National Geographic Expeditions puts on tours which include three days in the cloud forest followed by a week on the Pacific coast of Costa Rica aboard National Geographic *Sea Lion*, which can accommodate 60 passengers; she is often compared to a private yacht, calling at gulfs, peninsulas and islands only accessible by boat, finishing at Panama and through the canal. I was hooked.

As usual, at my bequest, Amelia had enquired of Lindblad whether, ancient as I am, the whole enterprise would be within my scope and not be too athletic. The best way to get there was via Madrid (two-hour flight and/or stop-over) and starting from Heathrow at the rather unappetising hour of 6.20 am. Then a connecting (so-called) flight to the capital San José (ten hours), which, alas, did not connect. So it is best to draw a veil over the very worst of modern travel and remember that this was an expedition.

Lindblad had arranged for the group to set out next day from San José to dine together and stay at the Hotel DoubleTree Cariari, so hoping for a jolly of sorts, I went to join them; the instruction had said 'you will gather for a welcome dinner at the hotel at 7 pm', so not knowing quite what to expect, I gathered. I found three tables each laid for about 15 people, with place labels and wine glasses at each place, which looked promising; no one appeared to be in charge to introduce anybody or even make a welcoming speech; Château la Pompe (water) was served in the wine glasses and this heralded dinner. Some of us bravely went to the adjacent bar to provide ourselves with a little flying speed, but it was a disappointing start.

The next day we set off in three minibuses for the five-hour scenic drive up the mountainous road to Monteverde Cloud Forest, the acclaimed private reserve, between 1,500 and 1,800 metres above sea level; the reserve was originally formed by a group of Quakers in 1951, who left America to avoid the draft. Buying land in Monteverde and clearing the forest for dairy farming, the community soon realised that the forest cover was essential to preserve the watershed and create the protected area of 541 hectares.

The road was good until the last hour or two, when it deteriorated, and the deforested countryside spread out before us in what looked like beautiful folds of heavy green velvet.

We stopped several times for short breaks and I swear that of all the many countries I have visited, Costa Rica has the most slap-up lavatories; shiny-tiled or stainless steel, you don't even have to pull the plug – it pulls itself! We were in our lodge by lunchtime and in the forest by 2.15 pm.

As luck would have it, there was no cloud that day, so with our exceptional young botanist Max leading the party of seven or eight, we progressed slowly through the immense 'gap colonisers' or 'pioneer trees'. These plants, he explained, were all adapted to make the best use of space and light, and thus increase their share of the major resources. It seemed they did this in a deliberate way, being either in competition with, or acting as sociable neighbours to each other. Tree behaviour is something I had not come across before I went to California, where it is very impressive: the seeds of those enormous redwoods frequently germinate too close to the parent tree and as they grow, they often need to fuse trunks or branches to hold each other up. Here in the cloud forest, these pioneers' first instinct would be to grow as big as possible, spreading out in all directions to claim all available space for themselves; others specialise in making the most of the very dim light, growing in the heavily shaded under-story in which most other plants would starve. Forest floor dwellers jostle each other for the sun flecks that slant down through the canopy; saplings of shade-tolerant trees bide their time, waiting for a forest giant or a huge branch laden with ferns, bromeliads and orchids to crash to the ground, crushing the undergrowth and opening up new space and light. Vast strangler figs (*Ficus ssp*) begin life as epiphytes (leaning on but not feeding off), often on an oak, of which there are about 15 varieties, expanding into buttresses as they progress; long roots grow downwards to eventually anchor in the forest floor, criss-crossing when they too fuse. The fig envelopes its support tree, constricting and shading and finally killing it.

Max was suddenly stationary – he could hear among other birdsong the rarely seen and spectacular quetzal; its fame had spread and I had hoped to see it when previously visiting Guatemala and Belize. Here it was, sitting with its exquisite back to us, high up among the branches, its curved ornamental tail feathers, iridescent green, white and red plumage, and showing off the long, emerald outer-wing plumes for which it is famous. Max found us other beautiful birds, among them the motmot and the red cardinal. What I really longed to see was the rare and silent tapir, but sadly it is among the interesting nocturnal creatures and not often visible.

I saw and photographed some interesting plants: *Hillia triflora*, with its red tubular flowers, are related to the coffee plant, which is grown commercially and very successfully in the north of Costa Rica; I also found many heliconias, which I love. Max found us a tarantula spider nesting in a bank; it was quite difficult to see but we did not take any liberties with it.

A whole day was devoted to the sky walk – a brilliant series of suspension bridges over the cloud forest canopy; it sounds hazardous, but it would be hard to fall off; the paths are made of nylon netting so you can see through, and they sway gently as you proceed; it is an amazing experience to walk over the tops of trees which are thickly thronged and magically silent. There were very few flowers, but one shrub, just within my grasp, had small pink blossoms and pink buds; I leant dangerously over to take a flower and a leaf as we had no guide to identify it. It turned out to be *Blakea grandiflora*.

The schedule included visits to two remarkable farms of butterflies and bats; we sat down to listen to a lecture full of interest on these mysterious creatures, though the extra talk on insects was rather too well illustrated, with large (about three inches), revolting cockroaches crawling all up and down our speaker, even in her hair – she seemed to relish them. We saw ravishing blue morpho butterflies with wide wingspans flop by in the soggy air, come to rest on a dead branch, fold its wings and disappear – impossible to photograph. I learned that bats usually hang upside-down by one leg only and even have babies in this unlikely position.

National Geographic *Sea Lion* was waiting for us at Herradura and we climbed aboard to settle into our rather Spartan small cabins; the shower/loo fitted into a space alongside the cupboard. Gathering in the lounge we were welcomed by the captain (who we rarely saw again) and his crew, and the excellent expedition team of Isabel, Gustavo and Max, who we already knew well. A glass of fruit juice accompanied this introduction.

Overnight we sailed down the Pacific coast to the wildest and most remote Osa Peninsula, only accessible by sea, foot or small aircraft. Here we could choose to go on nature walks (my choice), swimming from the beach, or horseback riding to explore further. After lunch we had another choice of the waterfall hike or stay on board, which is what I did, indulging in one of my usual shipboard pursuits – reading on deck. This ship was not ideal for this activity and the few available chairs were jammed close together and always occupied, a situation the rather unhelpful crew were not interested in improving. Those who went ashore had seen monkeys and a sloth.

Another 60 miles sailed before morning, we arrived in Golfo Dulce, where the Río Esquinas spreads its enormous estuary, and took advantage of the incoming tide to explore by zodiac as far upriver as time allowed. It seemed to be a wide delta with alternate river roads to choose from, all lined by marvellous mangrove forests of many different varieties. The tea or red mangrove dominates this area, but the black mangrove is also to be found; although it lives in this brackish water, it does not really enjoy the salt and has various methods of adapting to these adverse environments, such as storing it in old leaves which turn yellow and drop off. The roots provide both physical support and a mechanism for gas exchange, forming vast slow-growing formations. More strange roots hang down from the trunk to drink from the less salty surface water; there were pelicans and the occasional toucan to admire.

In the afternoon another treat in the form of Casa Orquideas, a private botanical garden created over 30 years by Ron and Trudy McAllister, an American couple who invited interested tourists to visit. Wonderful colourful orchids, heliconias, trees and birds, it was a marvellous couple of hours and I had to be dragged away to catch the boat.

Next day we sailed south towards Panama, to the Isla Coiba, which used to be the site of a federal penal colony for the worst sort of criminals. They are long gone, and the island is now a national park, covered in heavy virgin forest; rocky headlands project along the coast separating sandy beaches and mangrove swamps. An islet, Granito de Oro, provided the most heavenly swimming and snorkelling, in the warm, translucent, pale blue waters, round and in between the tiny islands swarming with exotic fish. A most amiable young man – our tour photographer – offered to kayak me over to the next island; this took three hours – luxury for me sitting in the back but hard work for him – but on arrival we were rewarded with a delicious barbecue lunch.

It was here that I had a great disappointment. Reggie, captain of my previous *Le Ponant* cruise, had told me his new ship would be likely to meet us at this very spot – and there she was! But owing to our indolent captain not giving me the message, I missed the opportunity for a wonderful visit to his ship from which he had offered to fetch and return me! I rang him from our bridge when I discovered what had occurred, but it was too late, and we lamented together what would have been an amazing meeting – ships passing, as it were, in the night.

Now on our way to the Panama Canal, we had one last chance of observing seabird colonies, which bred on the Isla Bona. The zodiacs took us close to the thousands of noisy brown boobies, who perched in rows among the shrubby trees, or on tops of rocks, or flew round in circles above our heads. The frigate birds showed off their elegance as they dived and plunged, pursuing the boobies.

They would not dream of breeding on the same islands as the common boobies; they force these seabirds to disgorge the fish they have just caught, which they then eat, and off they go to make their nests on their own exclusive atoll.

Crossing the Panama Canal was a wonderful climax to the expedition, and although I had traversed it during a previous cruise, I loved hearing the history of its construction and the detail of its operation once more. There was also an opportunity to visit the brilliant museum on the way to Panama City Airport, which made a fine end to an extraordinary adventure.

SOUTH AFRICA – A SEABORNE SAFARI

Africa is such a vast continent that I had only ever been able to visit a few of its fringes, such as Gibraltar, Tunis, the Red Sea, and one or two ports on the Indian Ocean. I was aware that South Africa had a huge variety of desirable plants, but most of them I could not grow because they required full sun, rarely available year round in Cornwall. So, as most of my travels are to investigate the habitats my plants enjoy, I had never given it much thought. However, when I was invited to stay with friends of a friend in Cape Town for three weeks, I could not wait to accept, and rushed to find out all I could about our history of involvement in that sensational country.

It all began in the early 15th century, when King Henry the Navigator of Portugal sent men to try to chart the coast of Africa, and it was Bartholomew Diaz who discovered the Cape of Good Hope in 1488. Ten years later, Vasco de Gama sailed on past the Cape, sighting and naming Natal on Christmas Day; he then continued to India, thus opening up the great trade route to the east, and in his wake came other traders from Holland and England. The Dutch East India Company was formed to exploit the riches of the spice trade and their ships broke the long journeys to the Indies at Table Bay, where they filled their casks with water but found little else; the tribes of Hottentots and Bushmen who lived there were nomads who built no towns, but lived travelling in search of game and grazing for their cattle.

The Company decided to make a settlement at the Cape, and Jan van Riebeeck was sent out to establish it; he took his wife and 90 men and they set about building a fort, growing a garden and making contact with the Hottentots with whom they hoped to barter. He was the first to find wonderful indigenous trees such as the yellowwood (*Podocarpus latifolius*), ironwood (*Olea capensis*) and, above all, the silver tree (*Leucodendron argenteum*), unique to the country and the now famous proteas and heaths of the fynbos. If van Riebeeck could have looked forward 40 years, he would have seen the garden – which he cut out of the bare veldt and cultivated in the teeth of shrieking southeasters, of floods that swept his seedlings into the sea, of parching droughts and devouring insects – become one of the wonders of the southern world. It is still just possible to identify the old garden in Cape Town which he planned and laid out 270 years ago. The Cape of Good Hope was ceded to Britain by the Dutch in 1814.

But how to get there? Flying direct was too boring; I would try and find a ship from which I could visit Saint Helena on the way. It was not as easy as I thought. There seemed to be no ships plying to and fro as one imagined. Banana boats used to take people but these had disappeared as well. There was one ship which could take me from Amsterdam to the Cape but I would be the only passenger and it did not stop at Saint Helena. The only ships that take people these days are cruise ships, so I found one which I could pick up in Namibia (where on earth was that?). *Corinthian II* was her name and she would take me from there via all the touristy places in South Africa to Richards Bay (just south of Mozambique), from where I could fly back to Cape Town.

I discovered that Namibia was quite an interesting country; it had been a German Protectorate from 1884 but was surrendered during the war in 1915, and became part of South Africa. It has rich mineral resources, with diamonds the chief export. The narrow Atlantic coastal plains of the Namib Desert rise to the central plateau, with the Kalahari Desert to the north and the Orange River as its southern boundary.

I flew overnight to Johannesburg, arriving at 5.30 am to catch a bus to Walvis Bay, the main port, where *Corinthian II* awaited. The weather was fine but far from hot. My cabin was okay and there was tea on arrival, followed by a long and interesting talk by the cruise director John. For dinner I noted in my diary that we had '*so called veal – resembled giraffe leg*' (can't think how I knew this as I do not remember ever eating giraffe). A very early start the next morning for our first excursion among the dunes. These are the most extraordinary ranges of huge sand hills on the edge of the Atlantic; the position of these dunes changes daily as the ferocious winds move them bodily from one location to another. We were taken in 4x4 Land Rovers and I sat in front with Danny, a sort of 18-year-old cowboy, thick as two planks but an intrepid driver. He drove at high speed up and down these amazing sand hills at perpendicular gradients and terrifying angles. I felt he was determined to frighten me to death as he drove faster and faster; luckily I rather enjoy this sort of thing and I gritted my teeth and hung on; I could see he had spent his life practising just this, so my hair did not stand quite on end. At last, at about 10.30 am, we arrived at Sandwich Bay, where two tents were erected for us and champagne and oysters were provided – these did have a calming effect. Here there was some very charismatic scenery, hills and dunes, and a very wide beach on the Atlantic with some rather exotic flamingos; the only other wildlife to be seen were geckos and occasional jackals. We paused on the return journey to see a large salt extraction area – this is one of the main exports and still belongs to an English firm.

Corinthian II – the cruise ship that took me round the coast of South Africa.

I decided to have a rest-day after this and attended two lectures, one on Namibia, which was good, and one on the explorer David Livingstone, even better; we continued sailing south round Africa, the coast of which I could see from my cabin, about 40 miles away. The wind was rather cold and there was nowhere nice to sit and read on deck, so I finished *Lucky Jim* comfortably in my bunk. The lifeboat drill was carefully carried out with the captain – four stripes and a beard – in charge.

Our arrival at the Cape gave us one of the longest and best days and included a ride in the cable-car up Table Mountain; it is an amazing feat of Swiss engineering but very dependent on the weather; we were lucky to enjoy it at its best, giving us time to admire the amazing views from the top and then catch it down again. Almost as soon as we returned, further trips were cancelled for the day due to strong wind. Table Mountain had once been an island but had become joined to the mainland by an area of low sand dunes called Cape Flats, so forming a peninsula, on one side of which is the cold Atlantic and on the other the warmer waters of the Indian Ocean. Buses took us for many miles round this peninsula, and we disembarked in a large car park from where everyone set out on foot for the penguin walk. On the way I found a delightful little beach much patronised by local families, and decided to sit down and watch the South Africans at play; it also gave me the opportunity to eat a particularly nasty boxed lunch, inedible except for some minute portions of brie and some water biscuits – quite enough for me. While I was waiting for the penguin party to return, a friendly bus driver pointed out a very obliging penguin which had made its nest and laid an egg in it on the edge of the car park, so I was able to study it at close hand. Another long drive and then the next stop was Kirstenbosch Botanic Garden. It was much too late in the day to do justice to this famous and marvellous collection of plants where we had been allocated only 40 minutes, but I knew I would be coming back so contented myself by asking to speak to a botanist who would know if there was a plant of the Australian *Banksia coccinea,* a particular variety I wanted to see. I was lucky to bypass several ill-informed guides at the desk and contact just such a specialist, the charming Graham Duncan, who very kindly left his office and showed me personally where other banksias were growing; with his telephone number and a promise to help me in the future, I returned to the ship with the others. After a dry martini for recovery, there was delicious grilled sole and scallop fish cakes for dinner.

Sailing on we came to Stellenbosch, a very pretty, well laid-out white village, made into a museum of old Dutch architecture; contemporary furnishings filled the rooms and kitchens of the cottages – the ladies in charge wore period clothes. Oak trees were planted in squares and the timber, which was valuable for casks and barrels, was also used in the vine culture.

Simon van der Stel (1639–1712) was the first Governor of the

Cape Colony; he was a gardener and also a mighty planter of oaks; he issued a decree that every farmer was to plant at least a hundred, and it is recorded that by 1687, 50,000 young oak trees had been established; he also experimented growing vines from France, Germany and Spain. The gardens between the cottages were laid out historically as they used to be and filled with vegetables and flowers. It was all most attractively done.

After lunch we were promised cheetahs; at least one or two hundred were in a confined area, but in the corner was a tent where one particular cheetah was waiting to be shown off. Everyone gathered round in the boiling hot sun, and shortly this beautiful creature was led in; he had two straps round him but he walked in and lay down as if to sleep on his table; we were given a talk about taking off sunglasses and hats, as the cheetah could see his reflection, which might apparently upset him. Then two by two, the tourists were ushered into his presence and encouraged to stroke him as he lay there; his handler was at his head with his lead round his fingers, but the cheetah seemed totally docile and resigned to put up with this patting from the throng. I sat on a very uncomfortable step in the shade while all this went on and at the end was able to take his photo. I could not approve of such exploiting of a wild animal in captivity, but was cheered up at the next stop where wine tasting was laid on at a rather smart hotel, and we then returned to the ship.

There was a varied programme promised for the following day and we started late owing to a headwind which delayed the ship. I had looked forward to this outing as it promised ostriches, and I have always been intrigued by these monster birds which can't fly – it seems such a pity. Would they begrudge us the use of their beautiful feathers if they knew how we esteem and use them? Open vans were provided for our transport, and after a long drive we arrived at some caves, but I did not feel inspired to walk round them. At the ostrich enclosure I was disappointed to find the birds were all in cages, or enclosed in fields, no wild ones, nor chicks, as I had been hoping for. Two or three bedraggled ostriches were introduced to us and treated as sort of pets, a little of their lifestyle explained; they looked thoroughly bored by this sort of thing. Afterwards we listened to a lecture in the ostrich museum; a small group of them under an acacia tree were to be seen in the distance as we drove away but they were out of range for photographs. Rather a wasted day, and I did not enjoy a furious drive back to the ship through dreary country, arriving with just two minutes to spare before sailing time.

Now for Port Elizabeth, and here we were promised wild creatures of all sorts, so the long, uncomfortable drive through the same sort of unthrilling countryside should be rewarding, and eventually we arrived at Kruger Wildlife Park, which stretched out as far as the eye could see. Here we were given an even more revolting boxed lunch than usual – some sort of gravy spilling over the chocolate bar – but luckily included banana and apple which I ate before abandoning the box. We set off in an open, seven-seat, 4x4 vehicle with a local driver who gave 'parrot talk' details of animal life; but here at last we saw wonderful animals in the wild. The giraffes were most entertaining – several of them sitting down in a small group as if to have a picnic. I hadn't realised that they couldn't reach the ground to graze unless they spread open wide their front legs. Giraffes seem to have been badly designed, which shows when they get up and down in a most ungainly way. There were flocks of impala which travelled like the wind, followed by hundreds of wildebeest, impressive in their numbers. At last I saw lovely wild ostriches in big family groups, looking so relaxed and happy that it quite made up for the previous day. There was just one rhino cooling off, elbow-deep in water; he ignored us. We were driven at speed over acres of scrub country with quite big hills – a very bumpy ride over quite good tracks and not unattractive landscape – on our way back to the entrance. Then two more hours' drive on a good road back to the ship – but worth every minute. At last I had seen Africa's wild animals roaming free in their natural habitat. That night, our entertainment consisted of some local tribe doing a really terrible dance and yelling – probably very touristy but not my scene.

We were still at Port Elizabeth, and after an 8 am start our treat was to visit Addo elephants; I am mad about these creatures, though I have only really seen the Indian variety, which are not as large and have much smaller ears, but are more intelligent. My knowledge of these marvellous animals dates back to our visit as a family to Ceylon, where we broke the journey on our way back from Singapore. We allowed time to take the children to an elephant orphans' home in Colombo, where they were putting on a little display of 'follow-my-leader' round their big tent. Here the head elephant – always a lady apparently – was in charge of dealing out the rations, and every day she would deliver to her neighbours' separate pens, in strict pecking order, a big bundle of sugarcane – their favourite treat. I subsequently came upon more Asian elephants on a trip to Thailand, which I was visiting with the International Dendrology Society. That time we were shown how they assist in the river transport of huge trees. We were then allowed to ride on them for their return journey, four of us to a *howdah* on each animal, and when the river got too deep for them to walk, they would swim (being transported on a swimming elephant is quite a unique experience). I had taken the precaution of buying a 'hand' of bananas, which I intended to give the mahout for his clever elephant at a suitable moment; I am not quite sure whether I expected him to peel each one before offering them, but what I did not expect was that he would lean over as we progressed and hold out the whole 'hand' – peel and all – to the elephant's trunk, who swept it into his mouth in one fell swoop – very impressive and obviously a much appreciated tip.

Whether the African elephants have any parlour tricks I shall never know, because in spite of scouring their habitat for two and a half hours in a very uncomfortable, covered, ten-seater van, we

*The incomparable Asian elephant in comparison
to the African.*

only saw some warthogs, a tortoise, and just one sad, lonely elephant not doing anything interesting.

Port Elizabeth itself has some pleasant old houses dating from about 1820, built for the first English settlers, many now converted into flats and schools; it was called Port Elizabeth after a now long-forgotten governor's wife.

Before retiring, the cruise director sought me out to tell me that it was extremely unlikely that I would catch my flight from Richards Bay to Cape Town the next day, as the ship was going backwards! I had not met this freak behaviour before and asked him to explain – he said there was a very fierce current ahead of us which had dragged us back. Nevertheless the gods were on my side and I did catch it by the skin of my teeth and travelled to Jo'burg in a nice little Dash 8, where I changed into a nasty Jumbo, but got to Cape Town on time.

Here I was met by my host and hostess who had invited me to stay and we bonded immediately. They lived in Constantia – the nicest place to live in Cape Town – in a charming house with lovely garden. We had dinner on the terrace and talked of our mutual friends. My host Anthony has fruit farms, and his wife Mim is involved in everything and knows everyone of interest. They could not have been kinder, taking me personally or sending me with their chauffeur to all the libraries and gardens I wanted to visit, and to many places that would be of special interest to me. I had the most lovely time. I made great friends with the driver who came from Mozambique, and told me I should visit if I had time. He was the kindest man and came into every library with me to help me find what I wanted and get the photocopying done. My host and hostess' house was full of books, and I spent hours sitting in the garden reading about the history of the country. So much I didn't know and so much to remember.

I was especially interested in the extraordinary historic figure of Cecil John Rhodes (1853–1902) and we went to visit his cottage where he died and which is now a little museum. His legacy of Rhodes Scholarships were the only thing I really knew about him, but they are among his many memorials. He was the son of an English clergyman and went to South Africa for his health when he was 17 and made a fortune at the Kimberly diamond diggings. He was obsessed with the dream of a British-controlled Africa, from the Cape of Good Hope to Cairo. With the cooperation of the Cape Dutch, he purchased the mining rights from the Matabele, and as a result the British South Africa Company was formed by Royal Charter in 1889. The creation of Rhodesia soon followed. In 1890, he became Prime Minister of the Cape and completed the Cape-Cairo telegraph. Just before the end of the Boer War Cecil Rhodes died, and in his last will – he started writing his wills when he was 24 – he left his huge fortune to public causes and the estate of Kirstenbosch to the United South African Nation; at that time the Cape, the Free State, the Transvaal and Natal were still separate entities, so Rhodes' idea of unity was not achieved until 31st May 1910. In the meantime, Kirstenbosch had no occupant, and for eight years it was uncared for; no one tended the vines and fruit trees, repaired the buildings or cleared the paths, leaving pigs to root for acorns under the oaks. In spite of this, the avenue Rhodes had planted through Kirstenbosch and over Constantia Nek to Hout Bay survived, and the Moreton Bay figs, the camphor trees, and the oaks still line the road between his offices and the gardens of Kirstenbosch, where the wonderful Botanic Garden was at last established, and which celebrated its centenary in 2013.

Of course Mim arranged for me to meet the curator, who took me round in a buggy, giving me a detailed account of this historic and beautiful garden, dedicated to the growing only of plants indigenous to the country.

Another place Mim took me to was Simonstown, which until 1967 had been used as an important strategic port by the Royal Navy, with many of its ships calling there on their way out to or homeward from India and the Far East. We walked round by the harbour and near the entrance found and admired a remarkable statue of a very large dog who was called Nuisance. We were able to read how he became a legend among servicemen, whom he habitually joined for runs ashore. He came from England, a rather well-bred Great Dane, who might have taken prizes at Crufts had he not run away to sea early in the war, then deserted at the South African naval base. There he was adopted by the ship's company of the depot, HMS *Afrikander*, christened appropriately and rated Able Dog (AD). My husband John wrote about Nuisance in his memoir at the time:

> 'When I landed at the dockyard in Simonstown for my first afternoon's leave, I had not heard about Nuisance, so paid little attention to the large dog that joined the cluster of people at the bus stop outside the main gate, but I did raise an eyebrow when he jumped the queue and settled himself into a seat. At the railway station he was the first to alight and raced ahead of me onto

*the platform; it was only a suburban journey to Cape
Town so I quite thought I had seen the last of him as
he hurried purposefully through the barrier as though
late for an appointment. But I was wrong, as I discovered when I cut the last train home rather fine for
Nuisance had cut it even finer. He charged up the platform and the whistle went just as he took his seat, and
when relaxing, he looked round with the proprietary
air of a season-ticket holder. During the journey he
appeared to be checking the liberty men, like a master-
at-arms, especially any of them that seemed the worse
for wear, and these he made his responsibility; he took
it upon himself to prevent drowsy sailors from alight-
ing at intermediate stops and jumped up to ensure they
got off at Simonstown.'*

I was glad to see his valuable assistance had been remembered in
this way.

There was time for one more treat before I left for England,
which was to visit the only private garden in South Africa to have
been designated a National Monument. Old Nectar is the creation
and the property of the owner, Una van der Spuy, whose house is
described as architecturally one of the finest and best known gabled
houses of the old Cape type. She and her husband acquired it in the
beautiful Jonkershoek valley near Stellenbosch, 60 kilometres from
Cape Town, in 1941. The house was situated on the steep slope of
the valley and clothed in vineyards. There was no electricity and
no plumbing. Her husband was fully engaged in military duties in
Europe for the duration of the war, so it was quite a challenge for
Una to move from a well-equipped London house with her two
little boys, with the prospect of only occasional visits from her husband of a few days at a time until he returned after the war, intend-
ing to retire there.

Una knew nothing about gardening and had no books or magazines on South African gardens, but she was rescued by finding in a second-hand bookshop a copy of a book by an Australian author called Brunning, in which the author's wide knowledge and clear presentation of every aspect of gardening made it a most valuable reference work. She was determined that her garden, comprising about two acres, was to be romantic and peaceful and in harmony with the house and surroundings. In five years she managed, with the help of some Italian prisoners of war, to complete this unique effect with seven gardens, each distinct in style. Among these were fine trees, terraced lawns, a rose garden, azaleas in the woodland and winding paths to take you from one enchanted area to another.

As she took us round she pointed out that the gardens were partially hidden from each other, so you found a surprise round every corner. After our tour we climbed the steep steps up to the house, and Mim took a photo of us two ancient gardeners sitting on a bench as we enjoyed our conversation, which could have gone on for ever; Una told me how she had started to write a book about her garden when she was 95! She gave me a copy and inscribed it:

'How I have enjoyed these two hours together and look forward to our next meeting – Una.'

THE SOUTH
CHINA SEAS

Naturalists who cruise to Borneo are usually on the trail of monkeys. There are several desirable varieties to be found there but I made it quite clear to the Orion Expedition people that if there was a choice of places to visit, I would prefer to see plants. I don't really like monkeys; I am probably prejudiced, because I have never actually known one personally, but they do not sound attractive, and I believe they bite. The plant I particularly wanted to see was indigenous to Borneo – *Rhododendron brookeanum*; it was discovered by Hugh Low, who began his hunt for orchids for his father's London nursery in 1844 and came upon these spectacular tropical rhododendrons, naming this particular one after his friend, Rajah Brooke. I had found Low's diaries (1844–1846) recently republished and planned to take them with me to follow as far as possible in his footsteps.

For some years I had been growing Vireya rhododendrons in clay pots, confined for the winter to my cold greenhouse in Cornwall, but released to the garden terrace as soon as the weather allowed; they were particularly valuable for cheering up the glasshouse all through the darkest days of winter and, not knowing about seasons where they come from, bursting into flower all over again during the summer. I had been fascinated by them since I read that in their own country – Borneo – they often adopt the delightful habit of blooming in the tops of trees in tall forests, displaying their dramatic rainbow range of colours to perfection; they produce seed in great quantities, which is unique in having tails at both ends, thus doubling their chances of landing windblown on some suitable vantage point, where they can germinate in moss and lichen, caught in the cleft of branches. But I had never managed to find a plant of *Rhododendron brookeanum* to grow at home; I grew one or two of the species, which are deliciously scented, unlike the hybrids, which were easier to acquire, and among my collection were 'Pink Delight', which flowered all winter, 'Ne Plus Ultra', with long-lasting flowers of bright crimson, and 'Saint Valentine', with masses of small, scarlet bells.

I flew to Singapore in January 2012, and after a night in the Fairmont Hotel, which overlooked the Raffles estate, I took a taxi to the Singapore Botanic Garden. Thomas Stamford Raffles acquired Singapore Island for the East India Company in 1819; with the construction of his bungalow, an experimental garden was laid out in which he planted cloves and nutmeg trees, and these formed the foundation of the Singapore Botanic Garden and the flourishing spice plantations which dominated the island landscape for many years.

I had been lucky enough to arrange to meet the Director of the Botanic Gardens, Nigel Taylor, who had promised to take me round this enormous garden in his buggy, and our first stop was to see the National Orchid Collection, which boasts the largest and finest display of orchids in the world. Hugh Low would not have believed his eyes! I had never seen these beautiful plants being cultivated outside before; even in the West Indies they often seem to be under glass. But here, flourishing in the most abandoned way, almost as if they were in the wild, were acres of heavenly varieties never before seen – by me anyway. The largest orchid ever discovered had actually come from Malaysia – *Gramatophyllum speciosum*. Frederick Sander, known as the Orchid King – Queen Victoria had appointed him the Royal Orchid Grower – had heard of it, and was determined to have it on his stand at the Exhibition in Chicago. When it was collected from the jungles in Penang, it weighed one ton; it was divided into two, and one half was donated to the Singapore Botanic Garden, where it was reputed to have produced 3,000 flowers simultaneously. His own portion created an enormous sensation in Chicago, and later he presented it to the Royal Botanic Gardens at Kew, where it is said to be (and I believe still is) the largest orchid in Europe. Nigel took me to see this historic plant – now labelled 'Tiger Orchid'; to my chagrin it was not in flower, but on its label it said:

> *'The flowers of the Tiger Orchid are patterned in colours quite like a tiger's coat. It forms immense clumps which are probably the heaviest orchids in the world. The plant flowers once a year when the two-metre long spikes make a magnificent show.'*

Sander was an interesting man; he was born in Germany in 1847 and at the age of 16 came to England with half a crown (30p) in his pocket. When he was introduced to the orchid species, he decided it was to be his life's passion, and he was helped in his ambition from his first job as a nurseryman in Kent, where he met and married the owner's daughter.

There was hardly time to do justice to this wonderful garden, and all too soon I had to thank Nigel for his valuable guiding and say goodbye. He then helped me into another taxi and off I went to HarbourFront, where *Orion II* lay awaiting me. She was a delightful ship and my cabin was all I could desire, with plenty of space and light from the big window. The first passenger I saw also waiting on the quay was an elderly man in a wheelchair with his daughter to look after him. She told me he was also stone deaf; I wondered how on earth they would manage. I met some of the other passengers, all Australian, except for the doctor and his wife, who were English – all charming and welcoming. There was also a very interesting botanist from Germany. We were greeted by the cruise director and his team who feted us with champagne. It was an encouraging start and we sailed at 5 pm.

Our first visit ashore was to Kuching in the state of Sarawak; I noted from Hugh Low's diary that he had arrived there on almost exactly the same day in January that I did, only it was 170 years later. He describes the fortnight of endless, deluging rain he had to put up with – how lucky we were in comparison. *Orion II* had anchored some way offshore; the ocean here is very shallow, so we always had to travel some distance to visit the islands. We climbed aboard the zodiacs from the stern of our ship; there were always two crew members to help us on and off as, with rough seas, some of the elderly passengers not used to boats might be in difficulty. Sadly *Orion II* did not have swimming arrangements from the stern where we embarked in the boats, similar to *Le Ponant*, which would have allowed us many more opportunities to cool off. The River Sarawak runs inland from Kuching, and the main party of passengers was looking for Orang-utans, which are found only on Borneo and Sumatra; their claim to fame is in having longer arms than any other great apes. I was allowed a special tour of my own, because it was here up the River Sarawak that Hugh Low found his special rhododendron. He says in his diary:

> *I shall never forget the first discovery of this gorgeous plant; it was epiphytal* [attached to but not feeding off] *upon a tree growing in the waters of a creek; the head of flowers was very large, arranged loosely, of the*

> *richest golden yellow, resplendent when in the sun, the*
> *habit graceful, the leaves large; very high and large*
> *trees in damp forests are its favourite haunts.*

He was clearly entranced with this and the many other plants he found – *'at that moment I thought that nothing would be more delightful that to live and die a hermit there'*; the expedition was not so successful, I fear; I went up the river by boat, searching among the many flowering trees upon the banks, but no sign of its golden flowers; even so, Hugh Low's words gave me a strong feeling of excitement, and I was fairly carried away like him, and thankful that I had at least visited this magic place.

That evening we were invited by the Sarawak Cultural Theme Party to observe traditional ethnic customs before the splendid Malaysian Banquet with local dancing. There were a few chairs, but mostly it was sitting cross legged on cushions. The fairly unidentifiable food was handed round and we did our best. The dancing was very much what one might expect, though it became slightly wilder as the night wore on. Some of my fellow passengers joined in.

Another memorable day took us ashore across very rough seas to Bako National Park, established in 1957 at the tip of the Muara Tebas peninsula at the mouth of the Bako and Kuching rivers. Millions of years of erosion of the sandstone have created a coastline of steep cliffs, rocky headlands and stretches of white, sandy bays. Many of these features have been carved by sea erosion at the base of the cliffs into fantastically shaped sea arches and stacks with coloured patterns formed by iron deposition. Bako contains every type of plant life only found in Borneo, with over 25 distinct types of vegetation from seven complete ecosystems, including mangrove, mixed dipterocarp, padang and peat swamp forest. Needless to say, there were many kinds of monkeys, monitor lizards, plantain squirrels, otters, snakes, and – what really interested me that I had never heard of – Borneo bearded pigs. It was an hour's very bumpy ride in the zodiac; we were warned of slight showers but ten-foot waves was more like it, and in spite of wearing our polythene ponchos, we were soaked with spray from every angle. I couldn't believe the captain would let all us elderly passengers loose in such seas – a nasty moment when the engine faltered – but the crew was well up to it, and we arrived with no great damage at a pontoon where we disembarked without incident. The beach was surrounded with holiday chalets, and to my pleasure, wild bearded pigs were snuffling around, quite unmoved by our presence, and almost immediately I spotted two babies with their mother, who hustled after them. She had a wonderful beard, and I continued searching for Dad, who had the best beard of them all; he was very large but slim and elegant, as were his family, and of a rather attractive russet-brown colour. The generous numbers of all these animals satisfied everybody, especially such as me, who were searching for a particular unknown species. Another hour-long ride across the fearsome seas took us back to the ship for hot showers and necessary large drinks and dinner.

*Wild bearded pigs snuffling around quite unmoved
by our presence.*

There was an exciting visit to the Tanjung Datu National Park. Famed for its long-tailed, crab-eating macaques. I had been worried about being able to keep up with the much younger explorers and holding them back – but the English doctor and his wife encouraged me to go as I was most anxious to see this only original pristine forest. We set out from the beach up a very steep path on this guided rainforest walk. The trees were enormous, strangler figs with huge buttresses. I kept up with the first group, only falling over once. Then another rather elderly couple and I were turned back to the beach, when the going was beginning to get a bit rough; there we had the pleasure of a long, cooling swim while waiting for the returning zodiacs. Charles Darwin described this sort of forest as 'one great, wild, untidy, luxuriant hothouse, made by nature for herself.'

Among the many interesting lectures given to us by our cruise team – all experts in their own subject – one described the great efforts being made locally to stop the destruction of these few remaining old forests, which are being replaced by plants that produce the profitable palm oil. Our cruise leader gave us a presentation called 'Plundering Paradise', explaining his views of the oil's impact on Borneo – 'is it a Panacea or Pariah?' – and an insight into the driving forces that are occurring all over Borneo and what the future holds for this biodiversity hotspot.

One island we visited, Tanjung Kumik, had never, we were told, seen white people before. They put on a marvellous traditional dance performance to their kind of music, after which we walked round their pretty island, admired their children, who dressed in splendid costume, and performed for us again. Most of their houses were built on stilts and the tide coming in and out washed away their drains so it all smelt tolerably clean.

One day there was a zodiac trip up the River Sungai Similajau, famous for its birds, particularly hornbills. The most distinctive feature of a hornbill is the heavy bill supported by powerful neck muscles; they possess binocular vision, which allows them to see their own bill tip – like seeing one's own nose – and they also have particularly long eyelashes which act as a sunshade.

The children's marvellous traditional dance on Tanjung Kumik.

Six zodiacs with six passengers in each had seats arranged in rows, more comfortably than usual. The river was enormous and the zodiacs drove between the lush, green banks covered in beautiful palms and other vegetation. It was a three-hour trip and other zodiacs followed us with drinks. We stopped many times to photo-graph such of the wildlife as took our fancy.

Our visit to Brunei was of interest. The Sultan had been educated in Malaysia's premier school in Kuala Lumpur, and further private schooling in Brunei; he then attended the Royal Military Academy, Sandhurst. His enormous wealth is based on his country's oil and he has attempted to share this with his countrymen, who all have free education and medical services. There are no personal or corpo-rate taxes in Brunei. We drove by bus along the waterfront, which encloses the 'water village', Kampong Ayer, where the houses are on stilts; it stretches about eight kilometres along the Brunei River and is a well-preserved national heritage site, the largest of its kind in the world, with approximately 30,000 residents. The Kampong is over a thousand years old and is sometimes called 'the Venice of the East'. We visited several museums, but the one which contained all the Sultan's coronation presents was the best; a beautiful, very large, bright green glass vase was his gift from Her Majesty The Queen. We passed the floodlit mosque on our way to the restau-rant where we dined, then fought our way back to the bus during a heavy tropical rain shower.

Our last visit was the Klias Wetlands tour, by zodiac to the vil-lage of Menumbok, where a local bus took us to the wetlands. There we embarked on special boats which took us up the wide river. This is the home of the proboscis monkey, which is a reddish-brown arboreal known for its huge belly and extra large and long nose, reaching to seven inches in length. This is supposed to be attrac-tive to the females, who also have big noses but not big enough to compete. The nose also acts as a resonating chamber, amplifying warning calls; in moments of extreme agitation the nose swells with blood, which makes the warnings louder and more intense. I can't say any of this makes much difference to my feelings for the animal, still very negative, I fear.

We had a wonderful boat ride up the river, the banks of which were covered in luxuriant growth, hundreds of birds, all making exotic calls, and many other kinds of monkey, which were quite difficult to identify even with those noses.

After a noisy farewell party, which was extremely jolly – we had made such friends, not only with the passengers, but with the crew team, all based in Australia, who were so knowledgeable about these extraordinary animals, birds and plants – it was sad to think I should be unlikely to cruise with them again. Although the wheelchair passenger could not join in much of the cruise activity, his daughter said he had enjoyed the sea air and being in such interesting country. I admired his courage.

We all prepared to fly back to Singapore from Kinabalu Airport – a short easy ride. As we flew over the Grand Harbour of Singapore, I was astonished to see hundreds of ships lying at anchor; I discovered from my taxi driver that there are never less than 400 or so ships there, waiting to deliver their cargo of oil palm, collected from the local islands, where it is grown to replace the old forests. This is processed very cheaply and then sent on to the Middle East – not surprisingly the country seemed to be extremely prosperous. I had time to take a boat trip down the Singapore River, from where one could see the back of many of the old buildings such as the Post Office – now a Hotel – and the Raffles Estate. Having spent three years on the island all those years ago (1950–1953) it was interesting to see if I could recognise anything and a very restful way of seeing what remained. I must admit, I could not remember much that I saw, but one sight, never to be forgotten and which is certainly new, is an amazing life-size model of a ship. It seems to be balanced precariously on the top of an existing hotel, and though it is used, I believe, as luxury accommodation, it is not a thing of beauty. Next day I had a quick trip to Chinatown to do some shopping before preparing for the night flight back to UK.

CRUISING WITH FRED

I was persuaded to indulge the Fred. Olsen line with my presence when I heard that I could embark at and return to Southampton, thereby not having to hang about at airports. It took a bit longer to get anywhere but I love being at sea so this sounded good. Amelia, my travel expert who advises me on cruises, told me that this particular voyage was a 'BOGOF' – Buy One Get One Free! She explained when I asked what that meant that 'as well as your 26-day voyage, you could choose from a dozen or more short cruises, all sailing from English ports, and go for about a week to such places as Morocco, Bruges, or Copenhagen'. As I had no particular desire to do more than one cruise, I decided to give it to my grandson and his wife, whose wedding I was going to miss because I had booked with Fred in such hurry that I mistook the dates. I hoped my grandson would forgive my absence if I gave them the cruise instead. In his place, I reckon I would have thought it a good exchange. I was grateful to Fred for his generosity.

After my rather impetuous booking, I was bombarded with information and instructions and realised that I was going to have a very different experience to my more casual small ship cruises, which were usually limited to one or two hundred people; this one accommodated over 800 and was as busy with rules as a boarding school. I was quite unprepared for the large clientele of such a cruise, and although I had seen at a distance some that looked like floating hotels, and allowed for 5,000 or more passengers, I could not visualise existing among so many. When packaged holidays hit the headlines and flying became within everyone's financial reach, it was fashionable to have been everywhere, and rather like twitchers, once you had seen the species (or had been to a well-known venue), you added it to your collection and just ticked it off – 'Wednesday? This must be Brussels' was well understood. So arriving at the docks at Southampton comfortably by taxi, ready to embark, I found myself surrounded by an enormous throng of presumably fellow passengers, and wondered what I had let myself in for.

My first shock was to discover that no booze was included or even allowed to be taken in your luggage, and any smuggled aboard would be confiscated and only returned on your arrival home. No such thing as 'Duty Free' was known to Fred, who charged London restaurant prices in his dining rooms. Even if you went ashore and bought a bottle of gin you would be searched on your return to the ship, and once more it would be taken from you. I felt I must try and outwit Fred somehow – my naval background did not allow such profligate drinking.

We sailed down the Solent that afternoon. My cabin was quite nice, with a small balcony and lovely view of the sea – but no fridge or mini-bar. And in the shower room no delightful little bottles of shampoo, bath essence, and all the small luxuries one looks forward to – just a bottle of unknown soap fixed alongside the taps. I was feeling deprived already.

To cheer myself up I went up on deck to watch us sail down the Solent. There was still a fierce wind from Siberia so I needed my fleece-lined jacket. I was impressed when we properly went through the life boat drill, and was quite ready for action when, approaching the Needles, our captain announced from the bridge that we had already developed a steering problem; now I knew where my life jacket was, but luckily it did not come to 'Abandon Ship'. During the night, I wondered if we were going round in circles and whether I would wake up with the Isle of Wight still in view, but luckily we were on our way. The Bay of Biscay was grey, as it often is – not to say bumpy.

I had booked for second sitting dinner at 8.30 pm, so somehow I had to buy myself a drink to pass the time. There were numerous bars and I investigated a few to see what the prospects were of getting the better of Fred. I discovered that, although you were not allowed to buy a bottle of gin at a bar, you could order one from Room Service and it would be delivered to your cabin – it cost only slightly more than Waitrose; on my dressing table was a bottle of still water, which I was about to open when I saw attached a note from Fred saying it would cost £1.50! If I rang room service, however, I could have sparkling at the same price instead. So I ordered a litre of Beefeater gin, some ice and slices of lemon (which were free), and poured myself my usual gin and soda with lots of ice and lemon. Thus fortified, I decided to explore the ship to see if there was a lounge up forward in which I could sit, enjoy my drink, and admire the ocean waves I anticipated as we sailed westward. A very long walk, plus a long lift ride, took me to Deck 9 where I found the Observatory Lounge. The Filipino waiters cast disapproving glances and rushed to carry my drink for me as I progressed through the length of the ship and chose my seat with the best view. This long walk became my evening habit and I became quite skilled at holding my drink and handbag in one hand and onto the rail with the other – the seas I observed from this vantage point as we reached the Atlantic became daily more dramatic, and here I met the more enterprising members of the cruise. It was a slight problem to decide whether to sit down at a table already occupied by a couple or sit alone at an empty one. Sometimes a couple might invite me to join them, which solved the dilemma, and I made some interesting acquaintances. In the old days you would automatically assume that these would be a married couple, but cruising can be the perfect place for what are apparently called 'silver splitters', which means couples of 60-plus who were trying out a new relationship, so just in case you must avoid any such words as husband, wife, partner, and allow them to lead the conversation safely. I never seemed to find the same people again.

I spent a lot of the daytime searching for the nicest place to sit and read; the ship was so enormous that by the time you had chosen a suitable *endroit*, in the shade, not too surrounded by people, without a gale blowing, you would invariably discover that you had left your book or dark glasses, or something else vital, behind, miles below in the cabin. One day, coming down in the lift, I had a conversation with a very tall, interesting-looking man and discovered that he was a great friend of a friend of mine; 'I know who you are,' I said, and as I told him, his mouth opened to reply and the lift door closed. The end of a beautiful friendship, I thought sadly, but not at all; my new friend had done some homework and rang me in my cabin to invite me to have a drink that evening with him and his wife.

One of the 'boarding school rules' to obey was the 'uniform', explained as 'The Dress Code'. I quote:

> *'Daytime wear is casual, no swimwear in the restaurant; dressing for dinner is traditional, the style being informal, gentlemen wearing jacket and/or tie (lounge suit or sports jacket), and ladies smartly dressed. Formal evenings: gentlemen will prefer black tie with ladies elegantly dressed in cocktail or evening dress.'*

A daily dress code also described *'smart casual – stylish leisure wear – open neck collars please for gents and casual separates or summer dresses for the ladies'*.

Dinner was punctual at 2030 as soon as the early sitting was cleared; I found my table for the duration accommodated ten of us 'singles', as we were known, all ladies – mostly called Betty – and one brave man Peter; he was very nice to us all. He sat on the far side of the table to me, so it was some days before we were introduced – as it were. I could see he was taking the wine list seriously, so I felt free to do so also. I chose a white and a red costing about £17 each. These I hoped would last me a week. It felt rather self-ish to jealously guard these, but soon most of us had our bottles closely in view, labelled with name and cabin number. The waiters fussed around, trying to make us drink up so we had to buy more. The wine was good and the food excellent – masses of choice and five courses. The lady next to me was the most ravishing creature (I wouldn't dare guess her age): her hair was done on top of her head in a spiky manner. She wore a different and amazing dress every night, covered in spangles and/or sequins; she told me she had painted her earrings herself to match each of her evening gowns; she was a dancer and was travelling with another lady (very well upholstered), who could have been her mother. She seemed to be always able to eat all five courses, and if she noted something I had chosen that she liked the look of, she would order that as well – the waiters did not seem to mind. It was very surprising to me that, although we were on the same ship, I never seemed to run into any of my 'single' Bettys during the day, so at dinner we all had a lot of news to exchange – thus we all became good friends. One evening, a new and unknown lady sat down with us and told us how she had somehow had to change tables; we welcomed her politely, but when she calmly picked up Peter's bottle of red wine and helped herself to several good slurps, we were stopped in our tracks; Peter was frightfully polite but the sudden silence that greeted her actions must have surprised her, because she never appeared at our table again; in fact, I never saw her again, but as one rarely ever saw anyone twice on this ship, perhaps it was no surprise. I rather regretted our uncivilised reactions to this poor woman – it was all Fred's fault.

Some of the 'Bettys' plus the one brave man – Peter.

I was surprised that there was no captain's table and that neither he nor any of the officers ever appeared or fraternised with the passengers; it seemed common practice in other ships for each of the senior officers to head a table, and indeed for them to be seen touring the ship during the day. Very occasionally, a little posse of them would appear chatting among themselves as they strolled through the restaurant – this was the only time one ever saw them. On one occasion when this happened, I needed someone to complain to, so I pounced on one of the group and told them my problem. The night before, I had gone up to retire to my cabin and had found the door open and a strange man taking my clothes and shoes out of my cupboards and generally making himself at home. I had been amazed and called my cabin steward to find out what was going on. Apparently this man – who for some reason was barefoot, which annoyed me even more – was changing cabins, and seemed to think he was moving into mine. No one was as cross as I was or took my rage seriously, and I was left to clear up his muddle. So this seemed a good opportunity to bring my complaint to light. The interloper had dropped his passport so I could hand this over as evidence. I had a phone call from an officer next day who invited me to her office, where we had a conversation which ended in her presenting me with an undistinguished bottle of wine as compensation. Better than a poke in the eye, I suppose.

There was no 'singles' lunch; instead it was to be found in a variety of buffets. One by the swimming pool served only fish and chips, another mostly salads on the upper deck. On bad weather days, my favourite was at smaller tables in the main dining room, alongside the vast windows, from where one felt quite close to the huge pounding waves. There was a buffet with every kind of delicacy, especially of the fishy kind, prawns of enormous size, smoked salmon, salads, delicious puddings and fruit, followed by a wonderful array of cheese.

After dinner there was always some entertainment in a very big lounge called Neptune. Our team of Bettys and Peter would sit together and buy each other drinks, thus cementing our group. The *Black Watch* Show Company and Orchestra put on a variety of singing and dancing shows with occasional soloists, magicians, and one night a very successful Chinese dragon, who danced in the most convincing way. In spite of very rough seas, the entertainment was not cancelled – just curtailed sometimes, as the singers slid sideways with the ship. Afterwards on a higher deck, 'hosted dancing' took place, and a selection of partners were lined up; quite late one night, one of the waiters was persuaded to do a comic turn at which he was much applauded, being extremely funny with his silently suggestive actions. I never ceased to be astonished at the ever more glamorous garments sported by our Bettys! They all had new outfits for every night; I had often wondered who bought the extraordinary clothes which illustrate the fashion catalogues that come routinely through the post. My fellow passengers' luggage must have been impressive.

The first morning, by now quite rough, I noted the stabilisers were doing their stuff; I went down the stairs to find the banisters were adorned with (luckily so far unused) paper sick bags. On this deck, in a most enormous lounge, everybody was playing Bridge. This cheered me at once and I consulted with the lady in charge, a New Zealander called Diana, who advised me to join her 'Improvers Class', which would be starting shortly when her 'Beginners' had ended. This became my routine when we were at sea, and was followed by an invitation to join another three players, so every day after lunch, we practised some of the new conventions or whatever we had just learnt. I really enjoyed these days with the Bridge always to look forward to.

After six days at sea we arrived at Funchal, Madeira, and those of us who had booked ahead for one of the outings offered were hustled off the ship to join a bus. I would recommend Fred to invest in a buggy, which many of us would gladly have paid for to transport us the mile or so we nearly always had to walk to get to the bus. I had been rather dubiously watching hundreds of elderly passengers, many of them with Zimmer frames, wheelchairs, and oxygen masks, wondering how they would ever make the distance, but became much more concerned about myself – that first outing, I nearly missed the bus. I was delighted to find my bus neighbour was Peter from our dinner table. Our driver was also our guide, and there was a large notice you could not miss in his bus, which said 'Tips are allowed!' He was very voluble and jokey and full of interesting information, giving graphic descriptions of everything, frequently making wild Latin gestures, pointing out objects which necessitated taking both his hands off the steering wheel.

It was some years since I had visited the island and now it seemed to have enormous motorways everywhere, cable-cars overhead, and extra roads at various levels, which did not add to its attraction. Every inch of space on the green mountains was built on. Strelitzias and agapanthus (both native to South Africa) were in full flower; mimosa, African tulip trees, and lots of decorative plants cheered it up, but the buildings seemed all rather down at heel, the gardens uncared for. Our tour took us to Machico, the landing point of the first discoverers of Madeira, now an historical village with the oldest church on the island. Then onto Blandy Park, where the wonderful, very old camellia plants would have been at their best in January, now sadly over. Camacha was next, the centre of the craft industry specialised particularly in baskets, of which we were invited to admire over a thousand varieties. Here we sat down to tea and cake while one of their folklore dance groups – rather like Morris Dancing – came on to entertain us. As it was now about noon, I suggested to Peter that this was the perfect moment for us to indulge in a glass of Madeira wine, and I begged him to go to the bar and buy us each one with his Euros (which I would repay him!); I have always found it very hard to choose a suitable time for this rather sweet drink. He thought this a brilliant idea and all our neighbours watched us enviously. The dancing went on – and on – inevitably, but thank heavens for the Madeira. Eventually we returned to the bus and back to the ship for lunch.

Overnight the ship sailed for Barbados (after which we called at a different island each day) and here I joined a minibus on a trip which ended with a visit to one of the best beaches on the fashionable coast of Saint James. On our way we passed the well-known hotel Sandy Bay; there seemed to be a lot of properties for sale, mostly under the sign of Sothebys. Sugarcane still covered large tracts of the countryside, but tourism appears to have taken over the industry today.

Grenada is one of my favourite islands with its beautiful Saint George's Bay and wonderful beaches, always surrounded by very lush, steep hills, woodlands, gardens, plants and exotic birds. I remember on a previous visit sitting by the beach, when a friendly parrot came and sat on my shoulder. I think I made a mistake in joining the Rhum Runner outing, as the passengers were supposed to dance and limbo round the boat which was entertaining us with its rumbustious steel band. I climbed to the top deck and sat up there throughout the voyage, enjoying the wonderful, turquoise-coloured but quite rough sea. We were frequently offered ice-cold rum punches in plastic cups. The weather in the West Indies during these days lived up to its brilliant reputation.

Saint Lucia provided the star turn, as far as I was concerned, with its Rainforest Aerial Tram. To get there a minibus took a limited number of us through the capital town of Castries and up 2,000 feet into the mountains, where we were to join a sort of cable-car – eight to a gondola – and get a bird's eye view of mature Caribbean oceanic rainforest, nurtured by warm gentle rain and rich volcanic soil; these remarkable carriages glided through and over the tree-tops, where knotted and twisted woody vines wind up the trunks; dense thickets of surreal vegetation merge with cascades of lavender stars, orange bursts, yellow berries and white lace, which thrive on the branches of the flowering trees. An occasional humming bird would visit. Sitting at the back of this group, a guide would describe what we were seeing; where the gondolas turned round to make their return, they climbed another 30 feet or so, and we were able to see both Atlantic and Caribbean oceans from this astral view point.

The most beautiful place in Antigua is Nelson's Harbour, but as I knew it would be overrun with tourists – not least ourselves – I chose to indulge myself (paid for through the nose in advance) in a lobster and champagne outing, sailing aboard the Mystic catamaran to Deep Bay Beach for a swim. Then to Turner's Bay, our second stop, where one could go ashore and sit under a coconut tree; here on board, the crew served us the anticipated lobster and champagne. But in my experience, anything arranged by Fred will not be quite what you expect; lunch was slightly spoilt by the crew refusing to give us a glass of anything before lunch, so we had to wait until the tables were set up and laid, salad was made, and lobsters were reheated, while we all sat there with our tongues hanging out. Then, while lunch was served, lots of bottles appeared; it wasn't champagne, but it was French and cold and faintly fizzy, so we didn't complain, but funnily enough the bottles were only three-quarters the size of a proper champagne bottle and of an unknown name. We were given several refills – one is thankful for small mercies.

It was my first visit to Tortola and we were able to board a catamaran, moored for once at a marina almost beside the ship. This sailed out across the Sir Francis Drake Channel, crossing the paths of Drake, Columbus and Kidd, and the hunting ground of marauding pirates such as the fictional Long John Silver. We made several stops, the best being at Norman Island for snorkelling and swimming, which one could do straight from the cat using the very well-designed steps up and down. The sea is always memorable, completely transparent, of a perfect temperature, and with those incomparable pale blue shaded stripes. Later I could even swim from the beach. This is something of a challenge at my advanced age, and I have to make sure I have a bodyguard handy in case I can't get out (this time Diana, my Bridge teacher); one can become cast like a sheep in foreshore waves, unable to stand up! But all went well.

The Azores were our last port to visit, and the weather got colder as we went north; I had been there once before, years ago, when Concorde made a fuelling stop and we were allowed to explore the cockpit and watch the fourteen hoses fill her up. Concorde had been on her way to Barbados, but so much time was wasted as she flew up and down by request to show herself off, one might as well have stuck to jumbos. *Black Watch* tied up at Ponta Delgada and we set off by bus in a north-easterly direction through agricultural country, very green, tidy fields with cattle grazing. These Portuguese islands have a contract to supply Japan with the dairy produce and intend to export pineapples as well, acres of which we inspected growing under cover. Our route was to take us past some picturesque villages to Feteiras, and from here the route ascended towards Sete Citades, where lies the main crater of an extinct volcano. From the edge of this crater we were supposed to admire a wonderful view of the two lakes at the bottom, one blue, reflecting the sky, and the other bright green, reflecting the rich vegetation that surrounds it. Imagine our disappointment when a vast cloud descended on us and we could see nothing at all; the bus driver had great difficulty even following the road. He managed to take us down a hairpin route to the Antonio Borges Botanic Garden, which is famous for a wonderful collection of European and tropical trees. From there we returned to the ship.

The last few days, the weather relented, and we could bask in the sun before returning to Southampton, where the bitter climate we had endured all winter with the same old wind from Siberia was waiting for us.

Fred's ships are just too big to travel in by yourself. You need someone of kindred spirit to share and laugh at the many good and bad shocks you are committed to. If you are an observer of human nature, you can enjoy writing down your thoughts, but the completely lonely life you lead means you might not speak to a single soul for a month and no one would notice. It is a sort of solitary confinement.

SHALL I
HAUL DOWN
MY FLAG?

It is often a good thing to be prone to impulses, and it was one of these that made me decide to move from Cornwall and live by the Thames in London. I had lived beside it some of my time as a Wren during the war and had found it a joy to watch this famous and historic waterway, redolent with antiquity, alive with ships, boats constantly moving up and down, and in those days accompanied by those beautiful river barges with their magnificent red rig, weaving unconcerned through the busy river traffic, where steam gives way to sail, and foghorns and hooting add to the bustling atmosphere. If I could find a flat with a balcony overlooking the river, I could almost imagine myself permanently at sea.

My kind and indefatigable family set to, and within a year the Cornish house was sold and I moved into a flat which ticked every box. I had not expected the weather to be on my side as well, but whereas in Cornwall it never stops raining, London is usually sunny; now I am sitting on my balcony, the sun is out, and a few feet across a brick path lie the tidal waters of the wide River Thames.

*How I wish the London skyline opposite my flat was
San Gimagnano instead of similarly shaped ugly Fulham
skyscrapers...but at night I can but only dream.*

Every evening, as I watch the sun go down behind the row of houseboats across the water, I think of the sunsets I observed on deck from far horizons – waiting for the green flash. Here in our latitude, the colours change slowly, and once the golden globe sinks behind the yellow streaks, it turns to fiery orange, sometimes interlaced with dark clouds, at last disappearing behind the houses that fringe the distance; very often the Chelsea Old Church bells ring out as accompaniment. I must admit that there is one group of ugly modern tower buildings in view, which I have christened San Gimignano (see picture), but after the sunset, when the buildings disappear, the hundreds of lights start to come on, joining the nightly show, and each one has a long pink reflection in the water shining deep down to the riverbed. The birds are always up to something – cormorants flying very low in neat formation, honking geese making use of the tide as they sail towards their nests, herons visiting at low tide and shrugging the tiresome seagulls out of the way. Considering whether to take another cruise this winter occurs to me from time to time; my sort of ships are few and far between, the fashionable trend being to make liners bigger and faster than ever. Fred has taught me that these are not for me, though they are attractive to more and more people, whose idea of a holiday is instant entertainment all day and all night with everything laid on. Strangely I learnt more about another type of clientele who cruise from a BBC talk on the television than from my time on board; it was from an interview with the chaplain of the *Balmoral*, a sister ship of *Black Watch,* also belonging to Fred. He seemed to have his finger on the pulse as he described the attitude of the many frail elderlies who had saved up for years to do the four-month round-the-world trip on their retirement. He took a blessing service for several fiftieth and sixtieth wedding anniversaries; he cared for one terminally ill lady, who in the middle of the night had to be winched up to a helicopter – what a splendid way to go – and he also observed many blossoming romances – it was all rather touching.

Christmas is the danger time – I am very vulnerable to brilliant ideas at that season. Dreaded January is just round the corner; I only need one tempting advertisement, one heavenly suggestion from Amelia, and I can't resist making yet another plan, imagining the delight of those warm, turquoise-blue seas and the exotic fish which swim beneath in blissful ignorance of their special charm.

Subject as I am to impulsive action, I cannot foretell what the future holds. Perhaps I shall just haul down my flag and be thankful to have had such luck in not choosing to cruise with *Costa Concordia* – our modern-day *Titanic* disaster – but to find myself gazing through my full-length windows at the River Thames, which daily reminds me of my travels around the world in eighty years.

THE END...?